Light on the Gospels

A READER'S GUIDE BY
JOHN L. McKENZIE

THE THOMAS MORE PRESS
CHICAGO, ILLINOIS

Light on the Gospels

The material in this book appeared
in another form in the newsletter
SEEK: A Contemporary Guide to the Gospels

ISBN: 0-88347-065-9

CONTENTS

Note: All references are to *The New Testament of the Jerusalem Bible* which the author abbreviates as JB and which is published by Doubleday & Company, New York, New York. The abbreviation "Q" indicates the Qumran documents discovered near the Dead Sea in 1947.

Chapter One

INTRODUCTION TO
THE GOSPELS

What are the Gospels?

The Greek word *euangelion*, which we translate "gospel,"
is never used in the documents of the New Testament
which we call the Gospels. It signifies in the first place the
good news which Jesus himself proclaimed, the good news
of the coming of the reign of God. In the second place it is
the good news proclaimed by the apostles of Jesus; but this
good news is that the reign of God has arrived in Jesus
Messiah. The earliest version of this announcement appears in some New Testament summaries in forms as brief
as our own Apostles' Creed: ". . . who was conceived by
the Holy Spirit, born of the Virgin Mary, suffered under
Pontius Pilate, was crucified, died and was buried. He
descended into hell. On the third day he arose again from
the dead. He ascended into heaven and sits at the right
hand of God the Father almighty; thence he shall come
again to judge the living and the dead." The gospel of Jesus
is the proclamation of a person and an event, and the event
is the climactic saving act of God; it is not the exposition of
a doctrine.

Neither is the gospel a biography or a history. The fact
that the external form of the Gospels resembles a biography confuses readers. It is not immediately evident that
there is no parallel to this literary form elsewhere in the
world. And we should add that there is no parallel in
literature to the relations between the Gospels of Mat-

thew, Mark and Luke, which are called the Synoptic
Gospels. Yet even in Mark, the shortest Gospel, the statement of the Christ event goes much beyond the summary
form illustrated above from the Apostles' Creed. The
written Gospels are more than the proclamation of the
good news. What is the additional material?

It is obvious that the expansion consists of stories about
Jesus and sayings of Jesus. The earliest proclamation of
the gospel is reflected not only in the summaries mentioned
but also in the epistles of Paul. From the letters of Paul,
however, one learns no stories about Jesus and only one
saying of Jesus (1 Cor 9:14). His gospel was, as we have
said, the proclamation of the Christ event: the redeeming
death and the saving resurrection. The written Gospels,
however, show an early interest in the life and person of
Jesus beyond the simple saving event. This interest, it
seems, arose from the developing life of the Christian communities, both Jewish and Gentile, in Palestine and the
cities of the Roman Empire. Questions arose concerning
the Christian moral response to the situations of life in
Jewish or pagan communities. In all probability such questions were first answered by appeals to the oral traditions,
the memories of the teaching and example of Jesus as they
were related by those who had heard, seen with their eyes,
looked upon and touched with their hands (1 Jn 1:1).

This development can be clearly seen if the Gospel of
Mark is compared with Matthew and Luke. Mark frequently says that Jesus taught, but he gives very little of
the content of his teaching. One wonders whether he did
not know the content or whether he thought it was not
important; more probably he believed that the content of
the teaching of Jesus was totally found in the teaching of
the apostles and disciples. As we noticed above, the gospel
in the apostolic church became the proclamation of Jesus
himself as an event; and in this proclamation, apparently,
the teaching of Jesus was contained. But when Matthew
and Luke came to be written this simple identification was

no longer enough; thus both of these gospels were enriched with the sayings of Jesus.

Yet the development of the teaching about Jesus does not obscure the original character of the gospel as an oral proclamation. The proclamation had to be oral because the hearing of the gospel was an interpersonal encounter. The gospel, which was at first the recital of the Christ event, was believed to be a word of power. Its impact did not depend on the eloquence or the personal charm of the speaker; it was a charismatic word whose power was neither enlarged nor limited by the personal power of the speaker. The apostolic church believed that the proclamation of the gospel made Jesus a present reality to the hearer just as he had been a present reality to the disciples who knew him personally. Their own experience of Jesus gave them no advantage over those who knew him only by hearing the gospel. The disciples too had to respond to Jesus by faith; what they affirmed of him was not the result of experience and observation, but of belief in his word. A person who heard the gospel proclaimed was in the same position as one who saw Jesus effect a cure or heard him utter a sermon or a parable. He was challenged to believe.

One who heard the gospel, like one who had seen and heard Jesus, could not plead ignorance or innocence; and the conviction that the gospel left no one indifferent relied on the belief that the gospel was a word of power which could not be evaded. One was challenged to believe; if one did not believe, one was not indifferent but an unbeliever. One had encountered reality and denied it. One had been offered the fullness of life and had preferred death. One had met God and chosen the world. It is not easy to share or even to understand the apostolic church's belief that Jesus lived in the gospel, but certainly this was their belief. The power of the word was the power of him who was proclaimed by the word; and the response commanded by the word was a response of matching power, the faith

that could move mountains, the faith which enabled the
disciples to do works greater than the works of Jesus
(Jn 14:12).

The power of the proclamation is not seen in the written
Gospels; they are not interpersonal encounters. Nor are
they addressed to the world, as the proclamation was; they
were written in faith for faith. This does not mean that
their purpose was to confirm faith or to furnish apologetic
material for those who might have to defend their faith; it
was a part of the proclamation that it needed no defense.
The written Gospels reflect the desire of the early Christians to flesh out, so to speak, the personal encounter with
Jesus which the proclamation was. They wished to hear his
words and to see him in action; hopefully the power of the
gospel would be enlarged if one saw the source of the
power more clearly.

Why is there more than one Gospel?

Since there is only one Jesus, one may ask why there is
more than one Gospel. The answer to this question is not
entirely clear, and it will be treated to some extent in the
introductions to each of the four Gospels, where it will be
necessary to point out the peculiar characteristics of each.
From early times it has been recognized that Matthew,
Mark and Luke have a resemblance to each other not only
in structure, but even in details and often in the very words
of the texts. This gives rise to the "Synoptic Question,"
by which is meant the problem of the relationship of these
three Gospels with each other. We noted above that this
interrelationship has no parallel elsewhere in literature.
Ancient writers spoke of *concordia discors,* a discordant
concord. Were it merely a problem of agreement, the question could be answered by establishing dependence; were
it merely disagreement, it would be a historical rather than
a literary problem. The historical problem could be resolved only by determining which of the sources could be
established as the most reliable and measuring the others

by this standard. If this could not be done, the historical problem would be insoluble.

The problem is seen in the wide agreement (with disagreement in detail) of Matthew and Luke with Mark. Most of Mark is found in Matthew and Luke. But Matthew and Luke, both more extensive than Mark, often have agreement with each other in material which is not found in Mark. In addition, both Matthew and Luke have material peculiar to themselves. The literature on this problem is enormous, and any simple statement of the solution would be false. The solution most commonly accepted, with numerous variations, is that both Matthew and Luke used Mark but not each other, and for the materials common to both but not in Mark they employed another source. This source appears to have been almost entirely, if not entirely, a collection of sayings of Jesus. This explanation is known as the "Two-Document Hypothesis," the two documents being Mark and the other written source. Thus there is general agreement that Mark is the first Gospel; and, while it is difficult to argue with assurance, there is general agreement also that Matthew is second and Luke third.

The dependence of Matthew and Luke on Mark and on at least one other document leads at once to the question of the immediate witness of these two evangelists. As we shall see, this dependence makes it highly unlikely that the Gospel of Matthew could be the work of the apostle Matthew, or that the author of the Gospel is reporting his own memories. This should be in itself no problem, and it really is not. The first generation of the apostolic church was amply endowed with men who had known Jesus and who had shared the experience of discipleship. It is evident from the entire New Testament that Jesus was and remained the primary object of their attention and devotion. The Gospels were written from a store of memory and oral tradition which it is no longer possible to reconstruct or even criticize. We can be sure that the store was available, and that it was highly important to the apostolic church that the authentic Jesus and not something else would be proclaimed as the object of faith.

Are the Gospels faithful to history?

This does not of itself answer the question of the historical value of the Gospels, a question which must be asked and answered. The major question does not arise from any doubts of the honesty or intelligence either of the evangelists or of their sources, but from discordances in the Gospels themselves. It is impossible within the scope of this work to deal with all such problems in detail, but it would serve the reader poorly to pretend that these problems do not exist and that they are not real. One may illustrate from the passion narratives. Modern scholars generally agree that the passion recital reached a fixed form earlier than the other Gospel material. Given this presupposition, it is remarkable that four accounts of the same event can vary so much in details. Yet the Gospels themselves assure us that this is one sequence of events which the disciples could have known only by hearsay. The hearsay is evident in our Gospels.

Moving from the passion to other Gospel narratives, one may consider first the infancy narratives. Is it safe to conclude from the absence of an infancy narrative in Mark that the original traditions had no infancy narrative? Such an assumption makes it easier to explain the striking diversity in Matthew and Luke, and to treat the infancy narratives as reconstructions of scattered pieces of tradition rather than memories. Lacking any genuine account of the infancy of Jesus (an account which is lacking for almost every person), the devotion of early Christians supplied an account based mostly on their faith in Jesus Messiah and the use of some messianic passages from the Old Testament. We encounter in these accounts a type of narrative which is not and could not be the same type of historical narrative which we have in the passion narratives, for all their divergences in detail.

Once it is granted that the infancy narratives are largely creations of faith, and that when there was no very clear memory of what did happen, the passion narratives were in some details filled out by conclusions concerning what had to happen or ought to have happened, we have moved to the question of how much the Gospels have transfigured Jesus. It should be noticed that this is not precisely a question of whether they are faithful to the realities of history. We have said that they were written from faith in Jesus Messiah for faith in Jesus Messiah. They are concerned with the life of Jesus, a period in which scarcely anyone even thought of him as Messiah. It is normal not only in popular but even in historical memory to view a person in terms of his fulfillment, even when dealing with those periods of his life prior to the fulfillment. There is scarcely any person known to history who has not been submitted to this type of transfiguration, in which the fullness of the future is foreshadowed in childhood or adolescence. That such transfiguration leads to the distortion of events is a manifest fact of human experience.

That such transfiguration leads to a distortion of history itself or of the hero of the history is by no means such a manifest fact. Or if it does, then let it be said that an undistorted view of events and persons is not within the reach of history, scientific or popular. Our point is that Jesus by transfiguration need be no more distorted from historical reality than Julius Caesar or Abraham Lincoln. All three are distorted to some extent, but not so distorted that the reality has been lost. It is true that we have no account of Jesus written by scribes and Pharisees. The account would be hostile, but not by that very fact distorted. The historian would feel enriched if such an account were discovered; the believer might feel threatened, but if his faith is solidly founded the reality in whom he believes would emerge with greater clarity. It is indeed one feature of Gospel criticism, whether literary or historical, that the reality narrated in the Gospels tends to resist dissolution under extremely rigorous and hostile

criticism. It is precisely this *concordia* in presenting a real
and entirely credible person—speaking historically—
which preserves the Gospels as historical records.

The question of the historical values of the Gospels
should not cause the reader to wonder whether he is en-
countering the real Jesus. He may wonder whether he is
reading the actual words of Jesus or whether the events of
which he reads occurred exactly as they are narrated.
Neither of these questions has anything to do with the
encounter of the real Jesus. We have observed that the
Gospels themselves with their numerous variations in
detail assure us that the authors could not achieve historical fidelity in all details and did not attempt to achieve
it. They could present the Jesus in whom the apostolic
church believed, and they could assemble enough memories to preserve the "teaching" based on the words and
actions of Jesus. These memories were almost entirely
anecdotal; no one, it seems, preserved a connected and
sequential account of the life of Jesus. The evangelists
were governed by Mark's basic pattern (Jesus' ministry in
Galilee, his journey to Jerusalem, and the week of the
Passion) which is preserved in Matthew and Luke, but
disappears in John. Each of the synoptic writers shows
liberty in the distribution of the material within this
scheme.

Modern interpreters have done considerable work in
attempting to understand how the church modified or even
created sayings of Jesus to answer questions which he had
never answered. The life of the Christian in a large Hellenistic city presented problems which the Palestinian Christian did not experience. The apostolic church examined
its memories of the words and deeds of Jesus and presented sayings which answered these questions by deduc-
ing the answers from its memories. They did not believe
they were being unfaithful to Jesus or to history when
they handled problems in this way. Jesus had revealed a
way of life, and when the explicit answer to a question

was not found in his quoted words, it was found there in principle. They realized that Jesus had not taught the world to adopt the manner of life of a Galilean peasant. But since most of his remembered words had been addressed to Galilean peasants, it would be false to his teaching mission not to adapt them to a wider world. One does not wish to say that the modern interest in history is unimportant; but the reader of the Gospels must with their authors accept the belief that the authentic Jesus could be presented with less than perfect fidelity to history. Unless one takes some of the liberties which they took, Jesus as a person and an event may be confined to Palestine of the first century of this era.

Chapter Two

INTRODUCTION TO
THE GOSPEL OF MATTHEW

Did the Apostle Matthew author the first Gospel?

The first and the fourth of the four Gospels are attributed to members of the Twelve. The name Matthew appears in the four lists of the Twelve given in the New Testament (Matthew 10:3; Mark 3:18; Luke 6:15; Acts 1:13). The tax collector who was chosen to be a disciple is called Levi in Mark (2:14) and Luke (5:27) but there is no doubt that the hero of the story is the same man who is called Matthew and not Levi in the first Gospel (9:9). The identification of the tax collector with the Matthew of the lists is not explicit, but there can be hardly any doubt that this slender connection was the basis for attributing the first Gospel to Matthew; that is, it was assumed that the identification came from the one man who surely knew who Matthew was. Very probably the Gospel stands first in the canon because the earliest collectors of the New Testament thought it was the first Gospel written. Yet neither the priority of the Gospel nor its attribution to Matthew is accepted by modern scholars.

The authorship and the priority, however, were attested as early as 130 A.D. by a certain Papias, bishop of Hierapolis; but his evidence is not preserved directly. Eusebius, the church historian of the fourth century, quotes the writings of Papias, which he has seen. The sentence of Papias, much discussed since Eusebius, reads in translation: "Matthew collected the sayings (*logia*) in the Hebrew language and each one translated (or interpreted) them as best he could."

Irenaeus in the late second century and Origen in the third century also attributed the Gospel to Matthew; but they may have depended on the testimony of Papias. Irenaeus dated the writing of the Gospel as contemporary with the preaching of Peter and Paul in Rome, therefore before the year 68.

Eusebius, not the most critical of historians, did not think that Papias was very well informed nor of very acute intelligence; and, as we have noticed, modern historians have been no more generous to him. Nothing of what he says is true of the Gospel we have. It is not a collection of sayings, although it has far more of the sayings of Jesus than Mark. It is not a translation from Aramaic (which Papias meant by "Hebrew"). It shows no more traces of translation than Mark or Luke, and critics are sure that ancient translators were not skillful enough to disguise the Aramaic oral tradition which lies behind the written Gospels. Very few modern scholars defend the thesis of an original Aramaic Matthew; and if it existed, it was so substantially modified in translation that it has left no traces of its identity in the Gospel we know by the name of Matthew.

Matthew cannot be the earliest of the Gospels, and the same factors which argue against its priority argue against its authorship by Matthew. If Matthew does not depend on Mark as a source, then it is impossible to establish literary dependence anywhere. In the story of the call of the tax-payer, just the passage in which, in the hypothesis that Matthew was the author, a personal memory would be contained, there is seen the same dependence on Mark that appears in the other narratives. The one independent feature is the name Matthew. The author of Matthew is normally dependent on Mark and another source which he has in common with Luke; nowhere does he betray personal memory and personal experience.

Modern critics have not, however, answered an obvious question which arises from their criticisms: Why should the Gospel be attributed to Matthew, who is in no way distinguished from the rest of the Twelve in the Gospel narratives? And was it the intention of the author, in adding the name Matthew to the story of the call of the tax collector, to identify this Matthew as the author of the document? There was no compulsion to attribute Gospels to the Twelve; Mark and Luke were not members of the Twelve. The attribution of Gospels to apostles is characteristic of the apocryphal gospels, which the church rejected. So little is known about Matthew that there is no difficulty in postulating a tradition associated with him. Krister Stendahl has spoken of "the school of St. Matthew" without implying an association with that member of the Twelve. The obscurity of Matthew as a person is itself the best reason for believing that the attribution of the name came from some genuine association with the person other than authorship.

Matthew is often called the most Jewish of the Gospels; the phrase is not easy to define accurately and it needs some qualifications, but once we have discussed its meaning we shall have set forth most of the major peculiarities of Matthew as opposed to Mark and Luke. In the first place, Matthew knows more about Jewish beliefs, learning and practices than Mark and Luke, and he mentions them more frequently. He is deeply concerned with the "Law" and with the "traditions." He clearly and emphatically proposes Jesus as the Messiah of Judaism foretold in the Old Testament. Other "Jewish" features will appear as we turn to various details of the Gospel.

The Jewishness of the Gospel

On the other hand, the "Jewishness" of Matthew is counterbalanced by the unquestioned fact that he is the most anti-Jewish of the New Testament writers. In our nervous modern world it is necessary to define this as carefully as possible. Matthew's anti-Jewishness is not vulgar anti-Semitism; he does not exhibit this prejudice, and he gives no genuine occasion for it. His anti-Jewish position is theologically, not ethnically, based; it is an affirmation that Jewish belief and Jewish theology are wrong. He is concerned with showing by theological controversy that Jews have erred in rejecting the Messiah of Judaism. To him it is so clear that Jesus is the Messiah that he can explain the rejection only as the result of willful disbelief. His presentation of Jesus Messiah is for Jews, not for Gentiles; his interest in Bible, Law and traditions comes from his desire to show unbelieving Jews that their own books and traditions disavow their unbelief.

If theological polemics are to be identified simply with anti-Semitism, then no discussion is possible. Matthew's thesis of willful disbelief is not essentially absurd or incredible; but it is an interpretation of events which is harsh to the persons concerned. The entire sequence of 21:28-46 reaches its culmination in the charge that the kingdom will be taken from the Jews and given to another nation. In the infancy narratives (2:1-23) foreigners come to worship the Messiah while the Scribes of Jerusalem, although given a clear biblical directional sign, remain in Jerusalem. The people of Jerusalem accept the responsibility for the death of Jesus when Pilate denies it (27:24). Matthew has made his own the pessimistic theology of Ezekiel (16 and 23), in which Israel was presented as unbelieving from the day of its creation as a people; Jerusalem has murdered the prophets (23:34-37). If, as most modern critics think, Matthew was written after the destruction of Jerusalem in the year 70, his thesis acquired weight from what Christians saw as the judgment of God on unbelief. They had not yet learned to identify themselves as the agents of God's judgments.

Matthew did not write his Gospel for Jews: he wrote it for Christians, and the thrust of the Gospel indicates that he wrote for Jewish Christians, that group which appears or is reflected in almost every book of the New Testament.

Historians are satisfied that a distinctly Jewish Christian group had almost disappeared by the end of the first century; there were no more Jews accepting the Messiah, and the form and style of the Christian communities were determined by the large majority of Gentile Christians. Matthew's Gospel can be understood as designed both to resolve doubts which might affect Jewish Christians and to furnish them with aids in controversy with Jews. Most modern scholars suggest that Syria is the most probable place for such Jewish Christian communities to be sought in the second half of the first century. Palestinian Judaism appears to have been nearly exterminated in the Jewish rebellion against Rome in 66-70. Matthew's knowledge of Palestinian Judaism does not recommend that we place him too far from this date in time or too far from Palestine in space. Antioch, the major city of Syria, furnishes the most likely place. No one would date the Gospel earlier than 55; the vast majority of commentators believe it should be dated after 70. And interestingly enough, Matthew knew Palestinian Judaism better than he knew Palestinian geography.

It is possible that the Jewishness of the Gospel is reflected in its structure, but this is not entirely certain. Many interpreters think the Gospel was arranged in five books, each of which contains one of Matthew's discourses preceded by a narrative section. The infancy narrative and the passion narrative are prologue and epilogue to the five books. The Gospel can be thus outlined:

Prologue: Genealogy and Infancy Narratives (1:1-2:23)
Book One: The Proclamation of the Reign (3:1-7:29)
    A. Narrative Section: The beginning of the Ministry (3:1-4:25)
    B. Discourse: The Sermon on the Mount (5:1-7:29)
Book Two: Ministry in Galilee (8:1-11:1)
    A. Narrative Section: Cycle of the ten miracles (8:1-9:34)
    B. Discourse: The Missionary Sermon (9:35-11:1)

The organization thus outlined is unbalanced; moreover, the invective against the Pharisees (23) is as long as some of these discourses. For these reasons some interpreters think the five-book division is fanciful. What gives this scheme fascination is the possibility that Matthew wrote his Gospel in five books in imitation of the five books of Moses, the "Law" of Judaism, and thus presented Jesus as the new Moses who proclaimed a new Law. The first of the discourses, which contains antitheses between Law and gospel, is delivered on a mountain as the decalogue was delivered on a mountain (Exodus 19-20). The presentation of Jesus as the new Moses who proclaims a new Law is clear in Matthew, especially in the Sermon on the Mount, but it does not depend on whether the Gospel is arranged in five books. Jesus draws antitheses between what "you have heard said of old" and what "I say to you." He is greater than the temple (12:6) and lord of the Sabbath (12:8).

Jesus commands faith as the Messiah of Judaism because he is son of God and son of David. The scope of this introduction does not permit us to explore fully the background of these two titles and their importance in Jewish messianism. In Matthew, the title son of God appears in the con-

fessions of the disciples (14:32) and of Peter (16:16) but it
does not appear in the parallel passages of Mark and Luke.
Matthew uses the title son of David more frequently than it
is used in Mark and Luke. By the first century the biblical
and Jewish idea of future salvation had come to include
as a conventional feature the restoration of the dynasty of
David under a descendant of David. This new David would
be a savior figure, as ancient kings had always been, but
the power of God would effect through him a salvation of
a novelty and a glory never seen nor expected. In Matthew,
though, Jesus does not really fulfill the idea of King Messiah, in spite of the theme of royalty which runs through
the infancy narratives. When Jesus is finally revealed, he
is not King Messiah but the suffering son of Man. He is the
savior of the poor, and he is one of the poor who knows
their sufferings. He can invite all those who labor and are
weary, for he himself is poor and lowly and he can comfort
them (11:28). He addressed the beatitudes not to the rich
and powerful but to the poor and the meek. His saving
activity will initiate the reign of God, not a reign of wealth
and political power. The reign is achieved by the free
submission of men to the will of God.

Matthew supports his polemic by a somewhat peculiar
use of the Old Testament. He has 41 quotations. Twenty-
one of these are found in Mark and Luke and may be
attributed to his sources. The remaining 20 must be attributed to Matthew. To him also must be attributed the
fulfillment formula, ". . . that it may be fulfilled. . . ."
Matthew uses this formula in a way not paralleled in Mark
and Luke. This does not imply that this use of the Old Testament was original with Matthew. It is now generally
agreed that the early Christians collected manuals of texts
which could be used to argue that Jesus was the Messiah
of the Old Testament. The texts peculiar to Matthew could
have come from such a *florilegium.*

The principle of "fulfillment" is difficult to define. It
certainly means more than the verification of a prediction.

In Matthew's classic phrase Jesus did not come to destroy the Law but to fulfill it (5:17). This can scarcely refer to the verification of a prediction. The phrase implies that the Law is in a developmental phase; it is not terminal. As we shall see shortly, this was a vital point of contradiction between Jesus and the Scribes and between Christians and Jews. Jesus fulfills the Law when he brings it to the fullness towards which in God's design it is directed. In the proclamation of Jesus this fullness is the reign of God. In Matthew and in the early Christian church the reign of God was identified with Jesus. The fullness of the reality of the reign does not annul the Law any more than mature manhood annuls childhood; but to remain in childhood would annul mature manhood. One must move beyond the Law when Jesus comes to reveal the full reality of the reign which was not revealed in the Law.

The reign of God as incarnated in Jesus is that full reality towards which not only the Law but also the prophets and the Scriptures moved; and it is in this sense that Matthew speaks of fulfillment. To think of his fulfillment texts as predictions verified compels to gross misinterpretations. Jesus is the Messiah son of David (1:22), the new and full Israel (2:15), whose identity as Messiah is indicated even by the name of the village where he dwells (2:22). He begins his ministry in the place where Isaiah saw the light of salvation dawning (4:15). He is the healer who releases men from illness (8:17), the compassionate Servant of the Lord (12:17-21). He experiences the unbelief which Isaiah saw in his own people (13:14). Israel had never experienced the fullness and the finality of the saving acts of God because it had never fully submitted to the reign of God. Now in Jesus the reign has come. The full saving act for which the prophets had prayed and hoped has come within reach. Jesus is not only the new Moses with a new Law; he is the new Israel, and it is here that Matthew's "anti-Jewishness" culminates. A new Israel is created whose members are not determined by descent from Abraham.

Even the descendants of Abraham must enter this new Israel, identical with the reign of God, by the same free act of submission exacted of Gentiles who enter it. The entire past—history, Law, prophets, psalms—is recognized as incomplete reality when the fullness appears; but those who know the early reality should recognize the fullness more easily than the Gentiles could recognize it.

Why is Matthew the most quoted Gospel?

Matthew is the most quoted of the Gospels and has been the most quoted from earliest Christian literature; and this is not merely because the Gospel stands in the first place and is therefore the most likely to be read or consulted. Matthew composed the sayings of Jesus carefully, and gave them that lapidary form which makes them memorable and quotable. The source of Matthew's sayings was more than the random brute memories of witnesses and those who had heard the witnesses. The sayings reflect the experience of the primitive church and the meditation of the church on the person and the words of Jesus. By the experience of the church I mean its apostolic and religious experience. I mean its answers to such questions as: How can Jesus be proposed most meaningfully to a different group without being unfaithful to his memory? What is an appeal to faith in Jesus, and how is it motivated? To what basic needs and desires does Jesus respond? How does his teaching touch this particular moral problem? How does one preserve Christian moral principles in situations in which Jesus did not live and for which he gave no explicit directions? Such questions were answered not by culling memories but by the formation of sayings which drew forth understanding not suggested by the sayings without the experience of the church.

A comparison of Matthew with Mark in the narratives is instructive. Matthew consistently abbreviates Mark's narratives, and he abbreviates by the omission of just those details which give Mark's narratives life and color. Mark, on the contrary, contains fewer sayings of Jesus and he takes no perceptible trouble to put them in memorable and quotable form. Between the two, it is obvious that Matthew is more interested in the sayings, Mark in the events. The interest in the sayings is most evident in the compilation of Matthew's discourses; we have mentioned the five major discourses, one other equally as long, and we have not mentioned the shorter discourses. One may compare the unrelated sayings of Mark and of Luke—who also arranges the sayings at times—to the book of Proverbs, and the discourses of Matthew to the book of Job. Unrelated sayings are not so safely preserved nor so meaningful as sayings woven into a discourse; the context both protects them from loss and makes them more intelligible. Matthew groups the sayings by such conventional techniques as the topic, the catchword and the numerical listing (seven woes against the Pharisees, eight beatitudes); some arrangements are more successful than others, but Matthew's intention to turn scattered sayings into lectures is clear.

Thus in Matthew Jesus Messiah has a feature which Mark and Luke did not recognize: Jesus is the Teacher. This is not evident in the use of the words "teach" and "teacher" or "rabbi"; all three Gospels use these terms. And while Jesus fell into no category of Jewish religious figures, the title "rabbi" designated him as one of a group which he resembled in his activity. But only for Matthew is the teaching a part of the messianic role and the messianic fulfillment. Jesus is not only the new Moses, he is also the last Scribe. Judaism knew both the Law (the text of the Pentateuch) and its interpretation (preserved in New Testament times only by the oral tradition of the rabbinical schools). Jesus proclaims with the authority of Moses and interprets with the authority of the Scribes; and Matthew accepts the Scribes as the heirs of the authority of Moses (23:2). It is equally clear that Jesus rejected "the traditions of the elders," not only in the passage where the phrase occurs (15:1-20) but also in several others, where topics like eating with sinners (9:10-13), fasting (9:14-17), the Sabbath observance (12:1-14), divorce (19:1-9), and other assorted obligations (23:16-25) are discussed. The fulfillment of the Law demands the annulment of the traditions.

The Jew, whether he was a Jewish Christian or not, would ask of Jesus the kind of authority which he knew in the Law and the traditions. Matthew presented Jesus as the new Moses and as the Messiah whose interpretation of Law made further interpretation impossible. In Jesus Messiah God revealed all that he had to reveal. Hence Jesus is presented in Matthew as a scribe fully equipped with scribal learning and scribal methodology. Examples of rabbinical dialectic appear in Matthew more generously than in any New Testament writer except Paul. Rabbinical dialectic is a distinctive type of argument based upon the Scriptures and upon a method of interpretation which assumes that a religious or moral truth can be deduced from any detail of the Scriptures. The methods can be seen in the discussion of the Sabbath (12:1-11), ritual cleanliness (15:1-20), divorce (19:1-12), the resurrection of the dead (22:23-33) and the son of David (22:41-46). Some of these, especially the two latter, may appear to be no more than *jeux d'esprit* to the modern reader; but the Scriptures were taken seriously in rabbinical dialectics, and the moral purpose was generally quite earnest.

Jesus had to be a Messiah of the Torah in the sense that he did all that the Torah did, and thus "fulfilled" the Torah. This does not imply that Mathew differed from Paul concerning the "annulment" of the Law by Jesus, for "fulfillment" and "annulment" here can mean the same thing with a difference of emphasis. Paul said that the whole Law was summed up in one commandment (Romans 13:8-10; Galatians 5:14). Matthew has the saying that the entire revelation of the Scriptures ("Law and Prophets") hangs on the two commandments of the love of God and the love of neighbor (22:34-40). The saying is a saying of

Jesus, and both Matthew and Paul surely reflect the attitude of Jesus. The rabbis counted 613 different "commandments" in the Pentateuch and discussed their
importance in terms of "heavy" and "light"; this is the
background of the question of the Scribe in Matthew. The
saying of Jesus reduces the 613 to two and annuls the
others. For the Jewish evangelist it was important that the
Messiah who could sum up the entire Law in two of its
commandments knew perfectly the Law which he summed
up and spoke with an authority greater than the authority
of Moses. Matthew did not intend to yield to what must
have been an element of Jewish polemic, that the Christian
gospel was a solvent of the morality of the Law.

Jews believed that the Law was a complete code of conduct revealed by God, and that the study of the Law pro-
vided the sure and correct answer to every moral question.
By knowing and observing the Law the Jew was assured
of good relations with God. The name for this condition
was "righteousness." Only in Matthew does Jesus say to
his disciples that their righteousness must exceed the
righteousness of the Scribes and Pharisees (5:20). The Law
established a minimum, not a maximum standard. Jesus
adds, not only in this part of the Sermon on the Mount but
elsewhere in the Gospel, the demand that righteousness be
achieved not only in action and omission but also in the
"heart," the area of decision in which character is determined. He who observes the Law can be like a white-
washed tomb, clean and bright on the outside but full of
corruption within (23:27-28). The Law did not have that
moral power which created a new inner man; such a moral
power appeared in the teaching of Jesus, who thus "fulfilled" the Law.

Matthew could agree with Paul that the Law became a
burden; it imposed an enormous and complicated set of
external obligations which did not achieve sure righteousness. In the Jewish Gospel the teaching of Jesus should be
a complete guide of conduct like the Law, but it should

achieve sure righteousness without imposing an intolerable burden. The teaching of Jesus did this by the commandment of love. Yet love, while a simple principle, was not so obvious a guide of decision as to need no study. Krister Stendahl, who attributes the Gospel of Matthew to what he calls the "school of St. Matthew," identifies this school as a group of Jewish Christian scribes. The teaching of Jesus replaced the Law, and they studied the teaching of Jesus as Scribes studied the Law, in order to reach moral conclusions which were not superficially evident. The Gospel was a handbook of morality which would replace the scribal "teaching," the "traditions of the elders."

When Matthew is compared to Mark, certain differences in the presentation of Jesus can be recognized. The process is best described as transfiguration, but it is difficult to describe it precisely without adducing more examples than space permits. In Mark, Jesus is Messiah and Lord, but he appears in his full humanity; we shall point out examples of this in the introduction to Mark. In Matthew Jesus rarely shows emotion, and he does not ask for information. We have observed that Matthew usually abbreviates the narratives he draws from Mark. This abbreviation gives the miracle stories a character which has been described as "hieratic recital." Compare, for example, the healing of the epileptic in Mark 9:14-29 with Matthew 17:14-21, and the healing of the woman with a hemorrhage and the daughter of Jairus in Mark 5:21-43 with Matthew 9:18-26. Matthew has removed not only all element of suspense, but also any suggestion that the feat was difficult or even unusual. By the somewhat ponderous designation of "hieratic recital" it is meant that the miracles in Matthew become almost ceremonial in character; they are done with ease and dispatch, and they hardly seem to surpass the expected. In Matthew as compared to Mark, Jesus has begun to acquire a superhuman and unearthly character. Were it not for the Gospel of Mark we should not know that Jesus was ever seen in any other character. We have

said in the general introduction that the Gospels were
written from faith for faith. Matthew exhibits a faith which
was farther removed from the historical Jesus than the
faith of Mark, a faith which put into the earthly career of
the Messiah Lord attributes which belonged to him as
Risen Lord.

The disciples also are tranfigured in Matthew. Mark
often refers to their lack of faith and dullness of understanding. Actually they do not appear much superior to
the unbelieving Jews in their appreciation of the true
reality of Jesus. But by the time Matthew wrote, the
Twelve had become the founders and pillars of the
church, the witnesses of the life, death and resurrection
of Jesus. Even when he retains almost the exact words of
Mark in which the dullness and incredulity of the disciples
are revealed, Matthew denies that they lacked understanding or faith. Compare, for example, the rebuke of Mark
8:14-21 with Matthew's version in 16:5-12. Matthew has
softened the rebuke by omitting the harshest of the phrases
in Mark, and ends the incident by an affirmation that the
disciples finally understood. Even more violent is the transfiguration of Mark 6:52 in Matthew 14:33; the lack of understanding and the uncircumcised heart in Mark become
in Matthew a confession that Jesus is the son of God.

The growth of both understanding and faith in the
Twelve is thus notably foreshortened. As we have noticed,
Peter and the Twelve are credited with confessing that
Jesus is the son of God in contexts where the other
evangelists do not have this confession. It must be admitted that Matthew has introduced a degree of unrealism
in his presentation both of Jesus and of the disciples. In
this respect he may be compared to Christian artists, who
have also put into their portrayals of Jesus a degree of
historical unrealism. Neither Matthew nor the artists did
this consciously; they wished to present in words or in
oils a portrait of Jesus Messiah and Lord.

The Gospel of the Church

Matthew is the only Gospel in which the Greek word *ekklesia,* church, appears, and it appears only twice (16:16; 18:17). It is for more reasons than this that Matthew is called the Gospel of the church. The discourse on the church (18) is the only treatment of church order in the Gospels; and it reflects the extremely simple order of the apostolic church. This order was not so simple that unbelieving and recalcitrant members could not be expelled; this happened in Corinth at a date earlier than Matthew. The missionary discourse (10) is also ecclesiastical; it is addressed to a church which is persecuted. The invective against the Pharisees (23) can be considered as a kind of anti-church discourse; it sets forth all the things which should not appear in the Christian community and in its officers. The Gospel of Matthew concludes with the commission to the Twelve to "make disciples" in all the world by teaching them the "commandments" (the law as a way of life) of Jesus; and thus the world wide church is conceived as built in the structure of Judaism.

Jesus comes as the prophet of the reign of God (in Matthew, most frequently the reign of heaven), and the phrase, found in all three Synoptic Gospels, has its peculiar uses in Matthew. One and the same reign can be described as a present reality, a reality to come in the future, and as eternal life. It is a present reality which is at hand or has arrived (4:17). It is eternal life which one who does the will of the Father will enter (7:22). The blessed sit down with the patriarchs to the messianic banquet in the kingdom of heaven (8:11; in such contexts "kingdom" is a more accurate translation than "reign"). As a present reality it is, in the parables of the reign (13), clearly identified with the church. It is the church founded by the proclamation of the word which can be suppressed or persecuted or can grow to fullness. It is the grain which is hampered

by the growth of weeds; both continue to grow until the
final separation in the harvest, and this is clearly the
church in its imperfection. It is a reality with small beginnings like the mustard tree or the leaven which grows
to greatness. Such a view of the reign-church, it seems,
could hardly have arisen until the apostolic church had
reached some maturity of experience. The church in the
world described in the parables is not a church which
expects the imminent return of Jesus as eschatological
Lord. The church is also the reign (or the kingdom) to
which Peter holds the keys, a reference to the ancient
royal officer called in Hebrew "the one over the house,"
the master of the palace or the major-domo. Eliakim,
major-domo of Hezekiah, carried the key of the house of
David (Isaiah 22:22). The church is not so obviously the
reign which one should seek with its righteousness (6:33);
this seems to refer to the submission to the will of God to
be accomplished concretely by submission to the teaching
of Jesus.

The ambiguity of the reign-church in Matthew is really
faithful to the ambiguous position of the church itself,
which is established as a bridge between the world of
history and the eschatological reign. In the church and only
in the church is the eschatological reign begun; the church
herself is manifest evidence that the reign of God is not
complete and perfect. The very idea of a reign of God
which is incomplete and imperfect is paradoxical; but it
should rather be called mysterious, for surely that reign
which begins with the violent death of him who announces
the reign has begun in mystery. The church as the revelation of the reign and its realization exhibits both its initial
and its terminal phases; and the believer can see the consummation of the reign in its beginning. Certainly he can
see its character established. For Matthew the reign is
recognized in the resurrection of Jesus as identified with
Jesus himself. This vision of the reign revealed in Jesus is
a part of the transfiguration of Jesus mentioned above.

Wherever two or three are gathered in the name of Jesus he is in their midst (18:20). And therefore the reign-church is identified with the group of disciples, with whom he remains until the consummation (28:20). This identification has a function in the transfiguration of the disciples. The reign in Matthew is world-wide in its scope; the Gospel is first to be proclaimed to the Jews, but in Matthew's view of their unbelief the reign has already been taken from them and given to a nation which bears its fruits (20:43). Even tax collectors and harlots push into the kingdom before the Jews (20:31-32). With Paul, Matthew affirms the saving value of faith against the Law.

Chapter Three

THE GOSPEL OF
MATTHEW, CHAPTERS 1–7

The Birth and Infancy of Jesus

Matthew and Luke alone of the Gospels have "infancy narratives"; these narratives, however, are independent of each other and in some details impossible to reconcile. *The genealogy of Jesus (1:1-17)* is, as commentators often remark, a sign of the "Jewishness" of Matthew; yet it should be noticed that no other biblical figure has a genealogy so extensive. The books of Ezra-Nehemiah shows that genealogies were important in the post-exilic community (Nehemiah 7:64-65). The first twenty-eight members which Matthew lists can be found in the Bible; the last fourteen come from an unknown source. The purpose of the genealogy is to show the Jewishness of Jesus (descent from Abraham) and his Messiahship (descent from David), hence it does not matter that some members are omitted.

The account of *the conception of Jesus (1:18-25)* is intended to affirm clearly the virginal conception of Jesus; nowhere in the New Testament is there any doubt of this early belief. The Messiahship of Jesus is again attested by his name, which signifies his character as savior, and his identification with the royal prince of Isaiah 7:14, quoted in 1:23.

The story of the Magi (2:1-12) and *the slaughter of the innocents of Bethlehem (2:13-23)* contrast the belief of Gentiles with the indifference of the Jews and the hostility of secular power, represented by Herod. The "magi" (wise men?) cannot be identified either by country or by profession. The recognition of Jesus Messiah by Gentiles, uninstructed in the Scriptures and led vaguely by a "star" interpreted by some unspecified lore, anticipates the theme of much of the Gospel of Matthew.

The infancy narratives as a whole can hardly be based upon authentic historical memories of witnesses. The episode of the Magi in particular is filled with incredible features. And it is scarcely possible that an atrocity like the slaughter of the children of Bethlehem would have left no trace in ancient historical sources, especially in Josephus, the Jewish historian whose writings cover the period in question. Josephus was profoundly hostile to Herod and relates the crimes of Herod with detail. The infancy narratives are to be classified as edifying legend akin to a type of Jewish religious writing called *midrash*. The purpose of the legend is not to report history but to affirm and illustrate a theological truth through a fictitious narrative. The theological purpose of the stories is clear and has been pointed out above.

In all four Gospel accounts of *the baptism of Jesus (3:1-17)*, the mysterious figure called "John the Baptizer" is a herald who announces the coming of Jesus. John is no doubt more mysterious to us than he was to the first generation of Christians; according to Acts 19:1-7, disciples of John could be found as far away as Ephesus, people "to whom faith in Jesus had never been proclaimed." Since the ritual washing which John performed was a symbol of repentance, Matthew adds the detail that John objected to baptizing Jesus; evidently the question of how Jesus could be baptized had been asked, and there was no answer except that "it is fitting that we should do all that righteousness demands" (3:15). The baptism becomes the occasion when Jesus is revealed as the son of God. The text invoked (3:17) actually has "servant" instead of "son" in Hebrew (Isaiah 42:1); an ambiguity in the Greek translation of Isaiah permits "son" to be used, but it is the Servant of the Lord who is recalled by the text. The subject of "saw" and the antecedent of "he" and "him" are ambiguous, but the words most obviously refer to Jesus. In John 1:32-33 they refer to John, but in the Synoptic Gospels the revelation of the baptism is directed to Jesus; he recognizes a new dimension of himself and his mission. With this awareness he begins—after a short preparation—to speak and act in public.

The period of preparation is the period of *the temptation of Jesus (4:1-11)*; both Matthew and Luke have an early expansion from the simple statement of Mark 1:13. The order of the second and third temptations is reversed in Matthew and Luke; Matthew seems to achieve a better climactic effect. The forty days in the desert suggests the forty years of Israel in the desert, no doubt deliberately; it also suggests the forty days and nights Moses spent on the mountain during which he fasted (Exodus 34:28; Deuteronomy 9:9). Jesus is the new Israel and the new Moses. The temptations are the temptations of the Messiah, but they also re-enact the temptations of Israel in the desert; Israel was tempted to rebel in its demands for food and drink, to rebel by challenging God, and to rebel by worshipping false gods. Israel fell, but the Messiah overcomes the temptations. The refinement of the temptations of Jesus lies in the invitation to employ his messianic power for vain display and secular domination. The tempter is refuted by sayings from the Law, the very book in which the temptations of Israel are related.

The Sermon on the Mount

In *a summary narrative (4:12-25)*, loosely connected with Mark 1:14-39, Matthew lays the ground for the delivery of the Sermon on the Mount. In the Gospel tradition, the beginning of the preaching of Jesus follows the imprisonment and silencing of John the Baptist; the hero does not take the stage until the herald has withdrawn. The groundwork is laid by the calling of four disciples and the attraction of attention by preaching and miracles. Matthew likens this beginning to the dawn of salvation in the birth of the messianic prince (Isaiah 8:23—9:7); Isaiah begins the oracle with an apostrophe to the regions of Galilee.

The *Sermon on the Mount (5:1—7:29)* is the first of the discourses characteristic of Matthew. It exhibits some structure up to 6:34; from that point it is a collection of unrelated sayings. In its present position it is intended to serve as a keynote discourse; and it does contain a number of radical Christian sayings. *The Beatitudes (5:2-12)* present a blunt inversion of conventional values; poverty, grief, righteousness, mercy, simplicity and reconciliation are congratulated instead of wealth, joy, moral license and power over others. The beatitudes identify Jesus with the masses of the poor of the Roman world and promise deliverance and reward to the poor and oppressed. The disciples are *the salt of the earth and the light of the world (5:13-16)* not only through their example but also by their proclamation of the gospel; see the parables of the mustard seed and the yeast (13:31-33).

The Jewish Law is dealt with in a *collection of antitheses (5:17-48),* with the Beatitudes the most radical statements of the sermon. The introduction (5:17-19) is possibly addressed to those Jewish Christians who believed that Paul and even Jesus had opened the doors to immorality; the "commandments" of Jesus bring the Law to perfection, they supply what the Law lacked. The righteousness of the commandments exceeds the righteousness of the Scribes and Pharisees, strict as they were. The six antitheses each propose a commandment (loosely quoted in 5:43) and show how the teaching of Jesus touches not only the external act but also the intention and the interior disposition. Morality does not consist in the avoidance of prohibited acts but in the desire of what is right. The sayings do not follow a consistent pattern; they vary between a revelation of the dispositions which lead to crime (as for murder and

adultery) and the prescription of actions radically opposite
to the crime. Thus murder is opposed by reconciliation, a
more sacred duty than worship; adultery is opposed to the
refusal of scandal, even at considerable personal loss (expressed by the exaggerations about the eye and hand).
Oaths, the legal safeguard against human mendacity, are
opposed to simple truthfulness. Revenge is opposed to
generosity beyond what is requested. Love of neighbor is
extended to all men; by loving one's enemies one ceases
to have enemies. Divorce is opposed to absolute and perpetual monogamy.

The antitheses have long been a Christian scandal; they
are usually regarded as exaggerated statements of an impossible moral ideal at which one aims but has no hope or
intention of reaching. Yet the sayings are as serious in tone
as any of the sayings of Jesus; and they leave no middle
ground between the righteousness of the Scribes and
Pharisees and the righteousness which enters the kingdom
of heaven. The specifically "Christian" moral ideal of the
gospel is found only in the paradoxes: anything else is
Jewish or Stoic.

The antitheses are followed by a collection of *sayings
about genuine and spurious righteousness (6:1-18)*. The
theme is illustrated from almsgiving, prayer and fasting;
and the test of genuineness is whether the actions are done
even when they are not observed. It is not the intention to
condemn all righteous actions which are done under observation; and there is no necessity for a lengthy explanation of actions done for display. The test may appear to be
excessively simple, but it is meant to exclude a very simple
and a very common component in human motives: the
opinion of others.

Into the discussion of prayer is inserted *the Lord's
Prayer (6:7-13)*; there is added a saying which comments
on the prayer of forgiveness, making forgiveness of others
the condition of receiving forgiveness from God. The form
of Matthew is the form used in worship and private prayer

rather than the shorter form of Luke (11:2-4). Of the seven petitions, the first three express a desire for the "eschatological event," the manifestation of God's judgment and saving power which ends history. The last four are easily understood as petitions for the basic necessities of Christian life, the help of God in material and moral need. However, according to some recent interpreters it is possible to understand the entire prayer as eschatological; the four petitions request admission to the messianic banquet, ultimate forgiveness, and escape from the eschatological temptations of the end of time (see 24:21-22).

There follows a collection of *sayings on singleness of purpose (6:19-34)*. Of these, 6:22-23 is general but somewhat obscure. The "diseased" eye is usually envy, and the original saying may have defined this vice as the vice which corrupts vision. The saying as it stands treats the eye as the aperture through which light enters; the diseased eye interposes evil. The other three sayings specify singleness of purpose in one area, the area of wealth. Worldly treasure is not lasting; it is a master whose claims rival the claims of God. The search for security is foolish because God alone can and does grant security. The recommendation to trust in God for economic security is, like the antitheses, a paradox which Christians have most frequently found necessary to interpret out of existence. The interpretation may be justified to some degree, for in the world in which the saying was uttered only the wealthy man could look beyond the present day; and Jesus is identified with the poor. But the saying does not mean that security is attained when everyone is sufficiently wealthy to provide for the morrow, or that a point is ever reached at which one need no longer depend on God. The saying must be taken in conjunction with the gospel recommendations to give to the poor; one of the ways in which God provides is by the generosity of men to each other.

Scattered sayings (7:1-27) comprise the remainder of the discourse. *Judgment of others (7:1-5)* is prohibited on the obvious grounds that the guilty are not entitled to render judgment. The saying about *dogs and swine (7:6)* is obscure and may be a popular proverb; it must refer to the proclamation of the gospel to those who refuse it. *Insistence in prayer (7:7-11)* is related in content to the sayings about trust in 6:25-34. *The golden rule (7:12)* is paralleled in the Talmud by a saying of the great Rabbi Hillel; the two sayings are probably independent, but 7:12 is not really a compendium of specifically Christian morality.

The sayings which follow have a certain community of tone if not of theme; they also have some eschatological reference. *The saying of the two gates (7:13-14)* is only approximately paralleled in Luke 13:23-24, and actually seems to answer the question which Luke evades; Matthew's saying is harsh. The saying about *false prophets (7:15-20)* is of general application; the sincerity of men's words is tested by their deeds. The saying no doubt reflects the experience of the primitive church. The same test of deeds is applied to all *the disciples (7:21-23)*; the deeds, it is explicitly noted, are not deeds of prophecy and miracles. It is admitted that these can be performed by false disciples; the true disciple keeps the commandments of Jesus.

The parable of the houses (7:24-27) affirms that security is found in the words of Jesus. The parable describes the house of mud brick, often endangered by torrential rains even if it is built on rock.

The *conclusion (7:28-29)* affirms the impression made by Jesus. The "authority" with which he taught, different from the authority of the Scribes, was the authority expressed in such phrases as "I say to you" in the antitheses. The Scribes sat on the chair of Moses (23:2); their teaching was validated by their membership in the scribal tradition, which was reckoned as going back to Moses and the elders. Jesus had authority outside this scheme; the Jewish reader would recognize that the only authority which superseded the authority of the Scribes was the authority of the Messiah.

Chapter Four

THE GOSPEL OF
MATTHEW, CHAPTERS 8–13

Ten Miracles

Matthew 8-9 is constructed to introduce the missionary discourse which follows; the narrative is built around ten miracles into which some sayings are interspersed. The number ten is not merely coincidental. Although most of the miracles are also found in Mark, one is found in Luke (Qumran), and one elsewhere in Matthew (the two blind men—see 20:29-34), Matthew has rearranged into a different order the miracles which occur in Mark, and no reason appears for this except that in the Bible the number of ten signifies completeness. The miracles include cures of leprosy, paralysis, fever, exorcism, blindness, dumbness, a resurrection, and a display of power over nature (the calming of the storm); and it is very likely that Matthew intended this to be a manifestation of the total miraculous power of Jesus. Since he wished a summary manifestation, Matthew abbreviated the narratives by the omission of descriptive details.

The significant points of the miracles, however, are retained. Thus in *the cure of the leper (8:1-4)*, the significant point is to be found in the parallel between the words of the leper, the response of Jesus and the execution of the cure. In the cure of *the centurion's slave (8:5-13)*, Matthew has omitted the intermediaries mentioned by Luke; the significant point is the contrast between the faith of the Gentile, who believed that Jesus could cure even at a distance by a mere word, and the unbelief of the Jews. Yet,

43

oddly, Matthew has not yet introduced the theme of Jewish unbelief. *The healing of Peter's mother-in-law (8:14-15)* and *the summary of healings (8:16-17)* are barely mentioned.

At this point, Matthew inserts two *sayings on discipleship and renunciation (8:18-22)*, found also in Luke (Q). These are preparation for the calling of the Twelve (10:1-4). The sayings demand renunciation of home and family; in fact, the first (vv.19-20) is understood to refer to the homelessness of Jesus himself. "To bury one's father" does not mean actual interment, but to live with the father and support him until he dies.

The miracles of *the calming of the sea (8:23-27)* and *the exorcism of the demoniacs of Gadara (8:28-34)* are abbreviated notably from Mark; and, strangely, Matthew has two demoniacs for Mark's one. The common element in both accounts, which Matthew emphasizes by his abbreviation, is the question of the identity of Jesus. The disciples ask who he is that he has such power (8:27), but the demons recognize him as the son of God (8:29). The cure of the paralytic (9:1-8) reveals another power of Jesus beyond his miraculous power—the power to forgive sins. Thus, both forgiveness and healing are granted in response to faith.

The call of Matthew (9:9-13; Levi in Mark and Luke) is really the account of a controversy which ends in a saying (9:13). The controversy concerns the association of Jesus with persons rejected by the "good people" of the Jewish community. The saying obviously identifies the "righteous" who are not called to repentance with the self-righteous.

The question of fasting (9:14-17) deals with a problem of the primitive church; Jesus had not observed Jewish fasts, nor had he treated them as obligatory. Fasting as a token of mourning was unsuitable in the presence of the messianic bridegroom, and this presence endures through the age of the church. The sayings of 16-17, originally unconnected with the question of fasting, affirm the same principle of the novelty of the Christian revelation.

The Missionary Discourse

Matthew transforms *the cure of the daughter of Jairus (9:18-26)* from a healing into a resurrection. In rewriting the story he has removed the rather crude idea of "power" flowing from the person of Jesus which Mark's account of the cure of the woman with a hemorrhage contains; the cure is effected not by the touch but by the word of Jesus. Evidently Mark was too crude for many in the primitive church. *The cure of the two blind men (9:27-31)* and *the cure of the deaf-mute (9:32-34)* are mere samples of the miraculous power of Jesus.

The missionary discourse (9:35—11:1) is prefaced by a note concerning the mission of Jesus and his compassion for the needs of the "crowds" (9:35-37); the passage actually looks to the institution and the mission of the church. The Twelve, who have not yet been called in Matthew's Gospel, are sent and enumerated. The instructions are not entirely "missionary"; they are rather general. It is a misunderstanding of the Gospels to think of any instructions as addressed to an elite. *The missionary instructions (10:5-16)* limit the mission of the Twelve to the Jews; this reflects the assured historic fact that the mission of Jesus himself did not go beyond Judaism, for Matthew more than the other Gospels recognizes the mission to the Gentiles. The preaching and healing are done without charge; the disciples are to live off the generosity of those who receive their ministry. They are to meet unbelief with simple separation from the unbelievers; it is assumed that the Jews to whom they speak are fully equipped to hear and to accept the message.

Sayings on discipleship (10:17—11:1), applicable to all Christians, complete the discourse. Persecution and family quarrels will be the result of the preaching; the disciples will fare no better than their master in this respect. The saying reflects both the memory of the passion of Jesus and the experience of the early church. Indeed, persecution becomes an occasion of the proclamation of the Gospel;

when the disciples are faced with persecution, the Spirit
speaks through them to their persecutors.

Sayings on fearless confession (10:26-33), well placed by
Matthew after the sayings on persecution, insist that the
disciples must speak what they have heard. The providence
of the Father follows them even into death, which is not
the supreme threat. To disown Jesus is to risk being dis-
owned by him in the eschatological crisis.

The division of families (10:34-36), already mentioned
in 10:21, is repeated more fully and strengthened by a
quotation from Scripture. This is a statement of fact, not of
principle, and it reflects the experience of the early church.
Nor is the later church without the experience that the
proclamation of the gospel of love and unity creates hostility and division.

Sayings on renunciation (10:37-39) carry this theme beyond earlier sayings in the Gospel. One must renounce
one's family, and life is rendered safe only by risking it for
the sake of Jesus. Not only death but the cross—the symbol of the most degrading punishment for the most debased
criminals—must be accepted; this reflects the history of
the passion of Jesus.

The conclusion (10:40—11:1) reinforces the authority of
the disciples. They are identified with Jesus because they
proclaim his gospel; they are empowered to preach in this
text, not to *rule.* The final saying expands the theme of
community to all works of kindness.

The general theme of chapters 11-12 is the incredulity
and hostility of the Jews. This is contrasted with *the witness of John the Baptist (11:2-19).* The question of John
affords the opportunity to affirm the works of Jesus in
language which reflects the Old Testament, especially
Second Isaiah, and to reveal the saving non-political
character of messiahship. Jesus declares that John is an
authentic prophet and the greatest of the prophets, but
that the reign which comes is superior to the entire past of
Judaism. The sayings of 11:16-19 may not belong in this

context; they are placed here because the name of John occurs. A popular proverb explains that Jesus could do nothing which would please those whose prejudice was firm.

Hymn of Thanksgiving

The doom of the Galilean cities (11:20-24), the scene of the ministry of Jesus on the shores of the Sea of Galilee, indicates that his preaching met a massive rejection. *The hymn of thanksgiving (11:25-27)* is pathetic in this context of failure; and it identifies the "mere children" with the disciples, and the "learned" with the Scribes and Pharisees (one may compare 1 Corinthians 1:26-31). The saying affirms a relation of Jesus with the Father which is not expressed elsewhere in the Synoptic Gospels, a relation of intimate mutual knowledge. *The saying about the yoke (11:28-30),* found only in Matthew, uses Jewish terms. The law was a yoke; the teaching of Jesus is not such a yoke. His teaching is comparatively easy because of its simplicity, and is intended for those who are "gentle and humble" (see 5:3-4), like the teacher.

The Sabbath controversies (12:1-14) revolve around self-help (12:1-8) and assistance of the neighbor (12:9-14). The questions are resolved in rabbinical fashion by an appeal to the text of Scripture. Objections to this interpretation of the Sabbath actually were raised only by the extremely rigorist wing of the Pharisees.

Jesus as the Servant of the Lord (12:15-21) is clearly identified by the quotation of Isaiah 42:1-4; this identification was vital in defining the character of the messiahship of Jesus. Oddly, however, Matthew seems to refer to the quotation here to the retirement of Jesus mentioned in 12:15.

The Beelzebub controversy (12:22-38) reports the charge that Jesus was in league with the devil; it is refuted by popular logic. To identify the very model of good works, the assistance of one in need, with the devil is to call the holy spirit an evil spirit; this is unforgivable because the blasphemer has denied the reality of the forgiver. The concluding sayings (12:33-37) probably come from another context; but they affirm the principle that a man is to be judged by his works.

In Luke (11:29-32) *the sign of Jonah* (12:38-42) is not associated with the resurrection, and Luke very probably has the original meaning, indicated by the context in both Matthew and Luke. Jonah is a sign of the prophet who preached to Gentiles who believed; Jesus preached to Jews who did not believe. ·

The unclean spirit (12:43-45) is also directed at unbelief. Jesus has repelled the kingdom of Satan, but those who do not believe will find that Satan returns to possess them more firmly.

The brethren of Jesus (12:46-50) are treated with a harshness which has been a stumbling block to commentators from early times. In other sayings about detachment (see 8:18-22; 10:34-37) it is clear that membership in the community of faith may demand the renunciation of one's family. The community of faith creates a new family for its members.

The Parables of the Reign (13:1-52) form another of the major discourses of Matthew; some of the parables he has in common with Mark-Luke, others with Luke (Q), and some have no parallel.

The parable of the sower (13:4-9) stands with no explanation; without the explanation given below (13:18-23) the reader is invited to search out the meaning. Many interpreters think it affirms that the reign will come in spite of all obstacles.

The revelation of parables (13:10-15) does not reveal but rather conceals the truth. The version of Matthew is less harsh than the version of Mark (4:10-12), but both quote Isaiah to illustrate preaching which has blindness as its effect. The passage is certainly difficult, but it can be understood as lacking distinction between blindness as the purpose of the parables and blindness as their effect. In the traditional wisdom of the ancients the riddle was not intended to conceal but to stir the listener to intense thought.

The faith of the disciples (13:16-17) is blessed in contrast with the blindness of the Jews.

The interpretation of the parable of the sower (13:18-23) is now generally regarded as the interpretation given by the early Christian community. It is an allegorical interpretation in which every detail has meaning; and in principle parables do not have allegorical interpretations.

The parable of the darnel (13:24-30) is peculiar to Matthew. To specify the weed as darnel, which resembles wheat, makes for a more likely version than those using "cockle" or "tares", neither of which has ever meant much to the English reader. *The parable of the mustard seed (13:31-32)* refers to the growth of the church from small beginnings. The figure is pressed; the mustard shrub is not the smallest tree, it is not even a tree; and it does not produce the smallest seed. It falls into the same significance as the parable of the sower. *The parable of yeast (13:33)* has the same meaning. *The parables as a form of teaching (13:34-35)* are justified by a quotation from the Scriptures.

The explanation of the parable of the darnel (13:36-43) is allegorical and thus probably the product of the early church, as noted above. But the parable admits no other explanation; and commentators generally think that both the parable and the interpretation come from the early church. This church experienced the presence of unworthy members, and it saw no solution to the problem except the eschatological judgment.

The parables of the treasure and the pearl (13:44-46), peculiar to Matthew, have the same theme. These alone are addressed to the individual person; they imply the renunciation demanded, but emphasize that the reward exceeds the renunciation. *The parable of the net (13:47-50),* also peculiar to Matthew, expresses the same theme as the parable of the darnel, and is to be attributed to the same source.

The conclusion (13:51-52) compares the parables to the wisdom of the wise man or the scribe; Matthew seems to have thought of himself as a Christian scribe. The parables are actually a formalized use of figures of speech, which can be couched in the form of a riddle. The reality of the reign is rendered intelligible by describing it in the language of common daily experience. The speech of Jesus in the Synoptic Gospels is anything but lofty.

Chapter Five

THE GOSPEL OF
MATTHEW, CHAPTERS 13–22

The Death of John the Baptist

The rejection of Jesus at Nazareth (13:53-58) is the occasion of the saying recorded in 13:57. This saying refers not merely to the people of Nazareth but to the entire Jewish people who have not honored the prophet whom the Gentiles have honored. *The account of the death of John the Baptist (14:1-12)* comes in almost as an appendix to the saying attributed to Herod (14:1-2). Matthew's account of John's death is shorter and less vivid than Mark's version (6:17-29); and Matthew adds that John's disciples told Jesus of the death (an addition which shows the desire of early Christians to associate Jesus with John).

The multiplication of the loaves (14:13-21) is abbreviated from Mark 6:30-44 in such a way that the symbolism and the anticipation of the Eucharist are heightened; compare 14:19 with 26:26. Both the feeding of the five thousand and the Eucharist are signs and symbols anticipating the messianic banquet (see 8-11-12). *The walking on the water (14:22-33)* is a singular episode in the Synoptic Gospels, and only Matthew adds the attempt of Peter to walk on the water. The symbolism of the disciples in the boat representing the church is obvious; Jesus is never far away, even when he cannot be seen. The attempt of Peter to walk on the water and his failure for lack of faith anticipates the commission given him in 16:18-19 and his denial of Jesus (26:69-75); Matthew indicates the special

51

position of Peter and his special problems. The incident is terminated by a *summary of miracles (14:34-36)*.

The dispute about cleanliness (15:1-20) is a controversy story ending in a saying (15:11) and its explanation (15:12-20). The passage no doubt reflects disputes in the early Christian community concerning the observance of the Levitical laws of cleanliness; the saying annuls these laws. There is now no "cleanliness" except cleanliness of heart (5:8). The dispute gives an occasion to contrast the merely legal observance of the Pharisees with the evasion of such precepts as honoring one's parents, interpreted in Judaism as supporting parents in their old age. This obligation could be evaded by consecrating one's goods to the temple (which removed them from profane use) while retaining the revenues.

The healing of the daughter of the Canaanite (15:21-28) emphasizes the assured fact that the ministry of Jesus was addressed only to Jews; but Matthew, the friend of tax collectors, sinners and Gentiles, does not mean that the disciples are to maintain the same limitation. The dialogue was not as harsh as it seems to modern readers, but is an example of ancient Near Eastern wisdom, which is displayed in the wit which matches riddle with riddle and wise sayings with wise sayings. The woman turns Jesus' saying to her own request, and is praised for her wisdom as well as for her faith. The account is followed by another *summary of miracles (15:29-31). The second multiplication of the loaves (15:32-39)* is clearly a duplication of the first (15:13-21); the duplication was already present not only in Mark but very probably also in the sources of Mark. The Eucharistic allusions appear in the duplicate (15:36) less obviously than in the first account.

Peter's Confession

The saying about the signs of the times (16:1-4) is substantially the same saying as 12:38-39. Matthew's account of *the leaven of the Pharisees (16:5-12)* is kinder to the

disciples than Mark's version (8:14-21), and Matthew adds
an explanation, which Mark does not have, referring the
leaven to the teaching of the Scribes and Pharisees.

The confession of Peter (16:13-23) is, in Mark's Gospel,
the first recognition of the messiahship of Jesus; Matthew,
however, has anticipated the confession in 14:33. Here also
only Matthew has added the confession of the divine sonship of Jesus. Simon is the first of the Twelve to recognize
Jesus as the Messiah. Again, only in Matthew is he given a
new name and a role indicated by the name; the change of
name from Simon to Peter is explained nowhere else in the
New Testament. The power to bind and loose in rabbinical
literature means the power to interpret the Jewish Law
both by imposing an obligation and by releasing from an
obligation; this power by itself would make Peter a kind
of chief rabbi. The holder of the keys was the major-domo
of ancient royal palaces. The phrase indicates the special
position of Peter among the disciples, sufficiently supported by texts in other books; it is left to the church to
determine the specific character of this position. The
position is awarded to Peter in return for his confession of
faith; the narrative immediately proceeds (16:21-23) to
evidence that the faith of Peter was imperfect, unable to
accept a Messiah who saved by his own suffering and
death. The rebuke of Peter is the sharpest rebuke given
to the disciples in all the Gospels.

Sayings on discipleship (16:24-28) pick up the theme of
suffering and extend it to the disciples, who must be ready
to renounce their lives, but with the sure hope of final
success in the renunciation. The sayings have already been
used in substantially the same form in 10:37-39; the reward will be granted in the second coming.

As far as the quality of the event is concerned, *the transfiguration (17:1-8)* has no parallel except the baptism. The
narrative has certain similarities to the revelation of the
Law on Mount Sinai, and the tents of 17:4 suggest the
Feast of Tabernacles, which in Jewish observance com-

memorated the giving of the Law. On this new mountain
of revelation the glory of the Messiah, normally hidden, is
revealed as the glory of the Lord shone through Moses on
Sinai (Exodus 34:29-35), and there appears the cloud
called "the Dwelling" (Exodus 19:9; 24:15-16), a symbol of
the presence of God. The Messiah, the fulfillment of the
saving act, stands between Moses and Elijah, representing
the Law and the Prophets.

The saying about Elijah (17:9-13) is attached to the
preceding by word association; only Matthew clearly
identifies John the Baptist as Elijah, but this is intended in
the other Gospels. In Jewish belief Elijah, who had not
died, would return to announce the Messiah.

The healing of the epileptic (17:14-20) is much con-
densed from Mark 9:14-29. Matthew calls the affliction
"lunacy," but as in Mark the affliction is attributed to a
demon; all commentators have recognized the symptoms of
epilepsy. The miracle story ends in a saying, but Matthew
has changed Mark's saying concerning prayer to a saying
about faith, very probably because Mark's saying was
difficult to understand. Mark's saying appears in 17:21,
but this verse is not found in the most trustworthy manuscripts. The miracle is followed by *the second prediction
of the passion (17:22-23). The saying about the temple tax
(17:24-27),* found only in Matthew, reflects the claims of
Jewish Christians to be free from this Jewish obligation.
The saying also associates Peter with Jesus and thus
echoes 16:18-19.

The discourse on the church (18:1-35) is an excellent
example of the composition of a discourse through successive word associations; and not all of the sayings deal
with the church. *Greatness in the kingdom of heaven (18:1-
4)* tells of the resolution of a dispute about rank. The
disciples are told to act like small children, in as much as
children could assert no personal rights. "Child" leads to
the sayings about scandal, first to little ones and then to
oneself; any sacrifice is demanded to avoid scandal, which

means placing an obstacle in the way of obedience to God. Care for the helpless is further recommended in the *parable of the lost sheep (18:12-14);* Jesus himself is the model of such care. The idea of care leads to the *sayings on fraternal correction (18:15-18);* these sayings are early illustrations of church discipline. The correction of the erring brother is a duty which lies upon the individual Christian. The matter is taken to the entire community only if individual correction fails; and the community is empowered to expel the unrepentant offender. The assembly in turn suggests *the assembly of prayer (18:19-20);* this assembly appears even if only two are joined in prayer. *The saying on forgiveness (18:21-22)* goes back to the saying on correction. "Seven" indicates a perfect number; the question asks how many times one is obligated to forgive in order to fulfill the obligation of forgiveness, and forgiveness is no longer required. Seven multiplied by itself signifies an indefinite time; there is never a point at which forgiveness is no longer required. This is emphasized by *the parable of the unforgiving debtor (18:21-35),* one of the most severe expressions attributed to Jesus in the Gospels, and found only in Matthew. The parable echoes 6:14-15, roughly paralleled in Mark 11:25.

The question about divorce (19:1-9) is a fuller treatment of the saying found in 5:31-32. Jesus is asked for an opinion concerning the difference between two celebrated rabbinical schools: Hillel permitted the man to divorce his wife "on any pretext"; Shammai permitted divorce only for adultery. Jesus permits divorce for no cause, and the obscure phrase "I am not speaking of fornication" (19:9), like the obscure phrase "except for the case of fornication" (5:32), does not make adultery a cause of divorce. The parallel versions of this saying in Mark and Luke permit no exception, nor is an exception understood in the saying which follows. *The saying on continence (19:10-12)* answers the disciples' remark that celibacy is preferable to an indissoluble marriage. The saying remarks that celibacy,

except in cases of physical disability, is a "gift" from God
not granted to everyone. The saying is found only in Matthew, and need not have belonged originally to the context
of the question of divorce.

Renunciation of Riches

The blessing of the children (19:13-15) is similar to 18:3.
The rich man (19:16-22) asks how he may possess eternal
life; Jesus tells him to observe the commandments of
Judaism. When the man asks for more, Jesus asks him to
become a disciple; the renunciation demanded is demanded of all disciples (10:37-39; 13:44-46; 16:24-26).
Wealth, however, keeps him from accepting the invitation.
The saying about riches (19:23-26) is a hyperbole which
should not be interpreted out of existence; it merely reaffirms the necessity of renouncing wealth in order to
become a disciple and to enter the kingdom. The reward of
renunciation (19:27-30) is pronounced in answer to the
questions of Peter concerning those who have made the
renunciation. The disciples could not have renounced great
wealth; the important point is that they renounced "all,"
whether it was more or less.

The parable of the laborers in the vineyard (20:1-16) is
found only in Matthew. It is open to more than one interpretation and very probably had acquired more than
one level of meaning before it was used by Matthew. The
most obvious meaning places Gentile Christians, the late-
comers, on the same level in the church as Jewish Christians. It may also signify that the early disciples, even the
Twelve, had no privileged position in comparison to those
who were called later. There follows the *third prediction
of the passion (20:17-18).*

The petition of the sons of Zebedee (20:20-23) exhibits
the failure of the disciples to understand the messiahship
of suffering; only Matthew introduces the mother as the
petitioner. Jesus promises suffering but no eminence;
compare 19:28. The indignation of the disciples introduces

a *saying on church authority (20:24-28)* in which authority is defined as service—literally slavery—to the members of the church; and Jesus, who delivers his life for others, is the model of this service. The ministry of Jesus outside Jerusalem is closed by *the healing of two blind men at Jericho (20:29-34);* here, as in the healing of the demoniac of Gadara (8:28), Matthew for unknown reasons has two men instead of the one mentioned in Mark.

The entry of Jesus into Jerusalem (21:1-11) introduces the last week of the life of Jesus. The action was a deliberate fulfillment of the texts quoted (Isaiah 62:11; Zechariah 9:9); the text of Zechariah clearly identifies the Messiah as one of the poor and lonely (see 5:3), and while it does not indicate a suffering messiah, it does remove the ideas of political power and pomp. Jesus then proceeds to *the purging of the temple (21:12-17).* The business was the sale of sacrificial animals, no doubt a concession of the priests, and Jesus removes from the temple this gainful activity. The next morning there occurs *the cursing of the fig tree (21:18-22);* Matthew has transformed a slow miracle into an instant miracle, and this in turn becomes the occasion for a saying about faith. The fig tree bore leaves but not fruit, and thus was a symbol of Pharisaic Judaism; the season has nothing to do with it.

Five Controversy Stories

The question of the authority of Jesus (21:23-27), is the first of five controversy stories collected here. By silencing the priests and elders concerning the authority of John, Jesus questions their competence to judge his authority. *The parable of the two sons (21:28-32)* clearly contrasts the obedience of the Christians with the disobedience of the Jews, and very probably reflects the experience of the early church. The parable of the wicked husbandmen is a very thinly veiled accusation that the Jews have killed the Messiah. This parable, with the punishment of the murderers expressly included, must reflect the experience of the early church in the form in which it is preserved. *The parable of the wedding feast (22:1-14)* presents the same theme of Jewish rejection and Gentile faith, although not even all the Gentiles accept the invitation. In Matthew's version this parable too reflects the experience of history.

The question of tribute to Caesar (22:15-22), the second controversy story, actually evades the question rather than answers it. Jesus does not intend to divide the world between God and Caesar. He points out that those who accept Caesar's authority oblige themselves to pay Caesar's price. *The question of the resurrection (22:23-33)*, the third controversy story, was a verbal trap, and Jesus handles it by a display of wit. The Sadducees accepted only the Law, and they are answered by a quotation from the Law. *The question of the greatest commandment (22:34-40)*, the fourth controversy story, is a typical rabbinical discussion; the rabbis distinguished "heavy" and "light" precepts and argued their relative importance, which could solve cases of conflicting obligations. The answer of Jesus, combining Deuteronomy 6:5 with Leviticus 19:18, would be judged by the rabbis as excellent. The additional remark (22:40) states the centrality of these two commandments in Christian morality; they are a compendium of all the commandments. *The question of the son of David (22:41-45)*, the fifth controversy story, is a verbal trap laid by Jesus. It shows that the Pharisees are unable to recognize the Messiah.

Chapter Six

THE GOSPEL OF
MATTHEW, CHAPTERS 23–28

Jesus' indictment of the scribes and Pharisees

The Jewishness of Matthew is evident in *the invective against the scribes and the Pharisees (23:1-36),* which has only scattered parallels in Mark and Luke; Matthew was addressed to Christians who were concerned about their relations with Jewish teaching. Jesus acknowledges the authority of the scribes (2-3), but finds faults with their indifference to the needs of the people, the difficulties which their teaching imposes, and their desire for display and respect (4-12). These sayings have been too rigorous for literal acceptance in the Christian community. There follows a sevenfold woe (13-32); allowing for some repetitiousness in the list, the complaints are that the scribes mislead their disciples, forbid virtue rather than encourage it, distort the truth by turning trivial obligations into serious ones and serious obligations into trivial ones, and mask their own vices under an edifying deportment. The last woe and the concluding lines (33-36) allude to the death of Jesus. The invective is intended as Matthew's final account of the words of Jesus to the religious authorities of his own community. The attitude of Jesus is not docile, uncritical submission. *The conclusion (37-39),* found in another context in Luke (13:34-35), reflects not only the failure of Jesus to make any impression on official Judaism but also the fall of Jerusalem in the Roman war in 70 A.D.

The eschatological discourse (24:1 through 25:46), the last of Matthew's "discourses," raises the question of the expectation of the Second Coming of Jesus *(Parousia)*. It is clear that many Christians of the apostolic age expected an early Parousia, and this belief is exhibited in a number of New Testament passages. At the same time such sayings as Matthew 24:36 reveal some ambiguity as to the time. This discourse refers both to the fall of Jerusalem in 70 A.D. and to the Parousia, but in such a way that the two events are not clearly distinguished. Both are exhibitions of the power and the judgment of God, and the fall of Jerusalem, a historical event when the Gospel was written, suggests the greater judgment of the whole world.

The prediction of the fall of Jerusalem (24:1-3) is followed by a question from the disciples concerning the time this will take place. The question is answered by the *signs of the Parousia (24:4-8)*, and the answer thus goes beyond the question. In fact the signs mentioned are simply the course of history. The same can be said of *the persecution and religious dissensions which are mentioned (24:9-14)*. The series, however, culminates in the proclamation of the gospel to the world, which precedes "the end." The discourse then returns to *the fall of Jerusalem (24:15-22)*; the emphasis on the suddenness is exaggerated and shows the merging of the fall of Jerusalem with the eschatological event, which will be sudden; see 24: 37-44. The *saying on false Christs (24:23-25)* is a fuller doublet of 24:5. *The day of the Son of Man (24:29-31)*, the Parousia, will follow "immediately"; the "sign" of the coming is the coming itself, and there will be no warning except the breakdown of the visible universe, described in images drawn from the Old Testament. The character of the imagery makes it clear that what is meant is a manifest vindication of the Son of Man, and that no picture of the event is drawn. The parable of *the fig tree (24:32-35)* is not clear, for the reader does not know what "these things" are which show that the Parousia is near. Thus *the exact time (24:36)* is not known even by the Son; this seems to be a correction of 24:32-35. When the Gospel was written, the "immediately" of 24:29 could not be taken literally. In accordance with 24:36, *a warning to vigilance (24:37-44)* emphasizes that the Parousia is sudden and unpredictable; Matthew plainly has preserved two traditions about the time and has not attempted to reconcile them. *The parable of the faithful servant (24:45-51)* can indeed be referred to the Parousia as a warning of its suddenness, but the parable has a different context in Luke. Its primary significance is not the Parousia but a warning to the officers of the church not to abuse their authority or to bully those whom they govern; see 20:25-28.

The parable of the bridesmaids (25:1-13) is peculiar to Matthew. Foresight rather than vigilance is recommended, but the application to the Parousia is clear, and the delay of the bridegroom is similar to the delay of the master in 24:49-50. The parable thus touches the ambiguity mentioned between an imminent Parousia and a Parousia indefinitely delayed. In both cases the return of the master and the arrival of the bridegroom can be expected in the "near" future; but because the event does not come immediately, both the unfaithful servant and the improvident bridesmaids act as if it will never come.

The parable of the talents (25:14-30) is found in another context in Luke (19:12-17) and does not refer directly to the Parousia; it is pointed rather to the assessment of one's personal achievement. This is not evaluated absolutely by some universal standard, but according to the potentialities of the individual person. It is not without interest that the penalty falls most severely on the person who manifests false humility; this is the man who, on the excuse that he is poorly endowed, accomplishes nothing.

The Last Judgment

The last judgment (25:31-46), as it is entitled by most interpreters, is a rather imaginative statement of the moral teaching of Jesus, and it has no parallel in the other Gospels. The scene is the Parousia before all mankind, but only the disciples are addressed. The traditional "corporal works of mercy" are enumerated in 25:35-36; it is on these and on these only that judgment is rendered on the disciples. The basis of the judgment is the identity between Jesus and the needy; the disciples are thus told clearly where they will find Jesus if they seek him, and how they must deal with him when they find him. The passage is an explicit commentary on the saying about the greatest commandments (22:34-40).

The passion narrative (26:1-27:66), as in all the Gospels, contains a fullness of details not found in any other part of the life of Jesus. This was the most important part of the earliest proclamation, and the first part to be incorporated in liturgical recitals.

The conspiracy of the Jewish authorities (26:1-5) is expanded and altered by Matthew from Mark (14:1-2) to show that Jesus is master of events; the event which the conspirators wished to avoid is predicted and does occur.

The anointing at Bethany (26:6-13) is found in all four Gospels; in all except Luke the event is an anticipation of death and burial. The praise of the woman's extravagant generosity takes some of the rigor off of the Gospel recommendations to give to the poor; love is not always discreet.

The betrayal of Judas (26:14-16) indicates difficulties in apprehending Jesus which the Gospels do not mention; together with the conspiracy this account suggests an attempted assassination rather than an arrest. It is doubtful that the disciples ever learned the full story of the deliberations of the Jewish authorities.

Judas' Betrayal of Jesus

Matthew's version of *the preparation for the Passover (26:17-19)* strangely suggests a simple prearrangement with no implications of second sight as compared with Mark (14:12-16)—strangely, for Matthew usually heightens the element of wonder. Matthew alone adds to *the prediction of the betrayal (26:20-25)* that Jesus revealed his knowledge to Judas; Jesus is master of events. Matthew's *institution of the Eucharist (26:26-29)* is closer to Mark than it is to Paul-Luke and emphasizes slightly more the sacrificial character of the rite (26:28). *The prediction of Peter's denial (26:30-35)* comes almost as a punishment for his vanity in claiming moral superiority over his fellows.

The episode of Gethsemani (26:36-46) follows closely the version of Mark (14:32-42). Matthew's account of *the arrest of Jesus (26:47-56)* has two notable expansions. The first is the address to Judas (50), now generally understood as an imperative ("Do what you came for") and not a question. The second is the saying against the use of force (52-54), which is quite in harmony with 5:38-42. Both sayings emphasize the theme that Jesus controls the events, even in his arrest.

The trial of Jesus (26:57-68) is a difficult passage which raises many questions; and it should be remembered that none of the disciples were present. Matthew follows Mark, but he abbreviates the narrative of the false witnesses and their failure to agree. It must be said that we have no certain and clear account either of the process or of the charge on which Jesus is condemned. The narrative assumes rather than proves that justice was perverted.

The denial of Peter (26:69-75) is again related, in dependence on Mark; Matthew introduces a second slave girl, like the two demoniacs of Gadara (8:28) and the two blind men of Jericho (20:30), and he alone adds that Peter was recognized as a Galilean by his dialect. Both the weakness of Peter and the forgiveness of Jesus were lessons to the apostolic church.

The delivery of Jesus to Pilate (27:1-2) contains a small but important rewriting of Mark. Mark most probably describes a mere assembly of the members of the council; Matthew turns it into another session, and there is no perceptible reason for this change. It is hardly likely that Matthew intended to add a daylight legal session to the

illegal night session. *The death of Judas (27:3-10)* is found
only in Matthew, and his version is at variance with the
tradition mentioned in Acts 1:18-19; there Judas himself
buys the field, and he dies from a fall and not from suicide.
Matthew does not intend to describe repentance but the
fulfillment of the saying of Jesus (26:24). Jews looked on
suicide with a horror unknown in the Hellenistic world;
in Stoicism it was recommended as an honorable escape
from an impossible position. The fulfillment text quoted as
Jeremiah is actually Zechariah 11:12-13, and it is now
generally thought that this attribution was made by the
source used by Matthew. The attribution may have come
from unconscious association of the text with Jeremiah
18:2-3 (the potter) and Jeremiah 32:6-15 (the field).

In *the hearing before Pilate (27:11-14)*, again dependent
on Mark, the charge is the claim of kingship; this was not
mentioned in the session of the council, and we again meet
a certain inconsistency in the account. *The sentence of
death (27:17-26)*, again following Mark, is not the description of a legal process; and we must again remember that
the disciples according to their own narratives were not
present. Matthew has added the legend of the dream of
Pilate's wife (27:19), the symbolic washing (27:24), and
the crowd's acceptance of responsibility (27:25). That the
process was determined by a mob scene has seemed unlikely to many historians. Others have asserted that the
Gospels attempt to shift the responsibility to the Jews from
the Romans. If the Romans executed Jesus with no Jewish
cooperation at all, then we have no knowledge of the
death of Jesus. Matthew does not excuse Pilate from guilt.
The narratives agree that Jesus was executed by a process
in which both Jewish and Roman authorities participated;
no more and no less than this is demanded by the evidence.

The mocking of the soldiers (27:27-31) follows Mark
except in the detail of the color of the cloak. Matthew
changes Mark's purple to red, which was actually the color
of the cloak of the Roman soldier. Kingship appears in

Matthew only in the infancy narratives and in the passion. *In the way of the cross (27:32)* Matthew mentions Simon but not his sons, very probably because they were not personally known to Matthew. In the narrative of *the crucifixion (27:33-44)* Matthew follows Mark closely, adding only the taunt that Jesus claimed to be the son of God (27:43). *The death of Jesus (27:45-56)* is dependent on Mark except for the wonders of 27:52-53, which must be reckoned as legendary. *The burial of Jesus (27:57-61)* is only slightly and not significantly abbreviated from Mark; but *the stationing of the guard at the tomb (27:62-66)* is found only in Matthew, and it is a necessary preliminary to 28:11-15.

In the resurrection narratives each of the evangelists goes his own way; yet Matthew's basic account of *the resurrection (28:1-10)* is dependent on Mark, omitting only the problem of the women concerning the removal of the stone (Mark 16:3-4). Matthew introduces an angel who rolls away the stone, and he has added an encounter of Jesus with the women.

The bribing of the soldiers (28:11-15), peculiar to Matthew, can be intended only as an answer to current charges that the disciples stole the body; both the charge and its refutation agree that the tomb was empty. *The apostolic commission (28:16-20)*, the last of Matthew's church sayings, is not paralleled in the other Gospels. The commission has a truly world-wide scope and emancipates the church from its Jewish background. The commission to baptize and to teach and the use of the Trinitarian formula reflect the mission as the church understood it in Matthew's generation. The closing verse expresses a belief closely akin to Paul's formula that the risen Jesus lives in the church.

Chapter Seven

INTRODUCTION TO MARK

Mark, the first of the Gospels

The Gospel of Mark stands second in the New Testament canon because of the assumption of the first compilers that it was the second Gospel. We have already seen that this assumption was false. Mark is regarded by scholars, with very few dissenters, as the earliest Gospel and the first written account of any kind about Jesus which we have. This does not preclude earlier sources which have not survived; but it does preclude an earlier Gospel. Mark, in fact, was the first to conceive and execute that account of Jesus which we call a gospel. It is evident that his is the shortest of the Gospels. A word count shows that Mark has about 50 verses (out of 661) that are not also found in Matthew or Luke. We have noticed that while Mark often says that Jesus taught, he does not give the content of the teaching. There are only two discourses: the parables (4:1-34) and the Parousia discourse (13:1-37). It is not surprising that early interpreters treated Mark as the least valuable of the Gospels; Augustine even thought that Mark was an abbreviation of Matthew. Modern scholars, however, have sometimes gone too far in the other direction and proposed that Mark, as the earliest of the Gospels, was the closest to the eyewitnesses and is the Gospel most free of expansion and transformation. Mark has also been credited with extreme simplicity, even naivete. Neither this nor his freedom from expansion and transformation can be affirmed. We do not need to move that far to show that for more than any other reason the importance of

Mark lies in the fact that he is the earliest literary witness to the life of Jesus. Matthew and Luke both employ him as a major source.

The author is universally recognized as the Mark who was the companion of Paul (Acts 12:25; Colossians 4:10; 2 Timothy 4:11; Philemon 24), of Barnabas (Acts 15:37, 39) and of Peter (I Peter 5:13). His mother had a house in Jerusalem where the disciples met (Acts 12:12). His association with Peter is also attested by Papias, bishop of Hierapolis in 130. Papias called Mark the "interpreter" (translator?) of Peter, and said that Mark wrote according to the discourses of Peter. Peter adapted his discourses to the needs of the audience, and Mark wrote the words as he remembered them. Thus Papias denied that Mark wrote "in order." Mark himself had not been a disciple or a witness of Jesus.

This testimony has raised much discussion, as we have seen from the testimony of Papias concerning Matthew. First, the question of order. The Gospel of Mark begins in Galilee and, after a few excursions to the borders of Galilee or barely beyond them, proceeds to Jerusalem, the passion and the death of Jesus. Matthew and Luke follow this same order of places in the life of Jesus, and most interpreters have thought that Mark represents the order of events as they occurred. Papias gives the impression that Mark's "order" was simply his memory of Peter's discourses. Some modern scholars think that the materials came to Mark with no arrangement at all—purely anecdotal—and that Mark himself created the arrangement. The conclusion would be that no memory of the order of events in the life of Jesus was preserved.

This contention, not accepted by most scholars, raises the question of whether the arrangement of Mark discloses any theological implication. A number of scholars believe that such an order can be discerned. X. Leon-Dufour, for instance, finds that the Gospel up to the confession of Peter (8:27-30) deals with the mystery of the Messiah, and thereafter with the mystery of the Son of Man. This arrangement is connected with the "messianic secret," which we shall discuss shortly. Other scholars believe that the purely geographical arrangement, whether it is historical or not, is all that Mark intended, and they deny any theological implications in the arrangement of the Gospel. No one believes that Mark was what Papias describes him as being, a mere collector or compiler. There is general agreement that there are theological implications in Mark's Gospel, and that they are quite subtle, subtle enough to permit his interpreters to disagree widely.

The account of Papias also raises the question of the sources of Mark. No written sources can be recognized. Nor is the view that his major source was Peter evident from the Gospel itself. The Gospel has a curiously colloquial running style, with many phrases like ". . . and then he went . . ." and ". . . and then he said. . . ." Added to this are realism and vividness in details, sometimes inconsequentially thrown in, like the fact that the daughter of Jairus was twelve years old (5:42). To some interpreters these traits have suggested the writing down of the oral recital of uneducated men. Others agree that this source is indeed suggested, but remark that the style is the style of Mark as well as his sources, and that these oral reciters need not be Peter or even the disciples. Perhaps it is most commonly thought that the source was a body of oral tradition already formed in the Christian communities.

This source is confirmed by the date and place usually assigned for the composition of Mark. There is a wide agreement that it was written about 65-70 A.D. This allows a thirty year period in which traditions of Jesus must have acquired some definite form even in oral transmission. As for the place, Mark was certainly written for Gentiles; and the ancient tradition that Rome was the place of composition, while it is not demonstrated, has not been abandoned. The readers of Mark knew Latin, which may argue Italy rather than Rome. Mark explains Jewish customs such as ritual ablutions (7:3-4), the date of the Passover supper (14:12) and the preparation for the Sabbath repose (15:42). He translates Aramaic words: *Boanerges* (3:17), *talitha cumi* (5:41), *corban* (7:11), *ephphatha* (7:34), *bar Timaeus* (110:46), *abba* (14:36), *Golgotha* (15:22), *eloi eloi lama sabachthani* (15:34). It is another example of Mark's realism that of these words only *Golgotha* and *eloi eloi lama sabachthani* are retained by Matthew, none by Luke. The prohibition of divorce includes the divorce of the husband by the wife, permitted in Hellenistic and Roman law but not in Jewish law (10:12). In 11:17 Mark alone quotes the entire text of Isaiah 56:7, "My house shall be called a house of prayer for all nations."

The details of a storyteller

Mark is less the theologian than the storyteller; and it is impossible within this brief introduction to enumerate all the details given by Mark which Matthew and Luke in parallel passages omit. This can be seen only by comparing the three Gospels where they narrate the same events. Most of these details are details of ocular perception, which do indeed suggest the memories of witnesses. We have alluded to such details as the use of Aramaic words; these are not likely to be the invention of folk reciters. One may say that the purpose of Mark was to present the "real Jesus," that is to say, "the historical Jesus." The Jesus of Mark did not command faith by his teaching; those who believed his teaching already believed in him. Faith was commanded by the presence of the person, who could be seen and heard and felt. It is a phrase of Mark (5:30), retained by Luke (8:46), that "power went out of him." It would seem that simply by presenting the sensible reality of the person, Mark presented the object of faith. This was the Jesus who said "Follow me," and men followed him. Mark, certainly, and his sources very probably, believed that if the storyteller could make that Jesus as vivid as he had been to those who encountered him, the same response would follow.

And this leads us to the celebrated problem of the messianic secret. The phrase was created by a German scholar, Wilhelm Wrede, in 1901. By the phrase he meant Mark's effort to explain the unbelief of the Jews. Wrede proposed that the Jews did not believe in Jesus Messiah because Jesus had never claimed to be Messiah. Mark, he affirmed, inserted the messianic claim into the life of Jesus but added that Jesus insisted that his messiahship be kept secret; hence the precepts to the disciples and even to demons not to reveal that he was Messiah. Wrede's solution does violence to all the Gospels, not merely to Mark; but the problem remains that Mark does have the precepts of silence. Matthew and Luke were not careful to preserve these because they did not understand this aspect of Mark. For them Jesus was the manifest Messiah; for Mark, in a sense, he was not.

A very human Jesus

A part of the problem is Mark's very human presentation both of Jesus and of the disciples. In the passage just cited (5:25-33) Jesus asks who has touched him. This was too naive for Matthew, who left out this detail; it was too naive for Luke, who makes Jesus explain why he asks the question. Only in Mark is Jesus angry (3:5) and indignant (10:14); only in Mark does Jesus wonder at the unbelief of the Nazarenes (6:6). Only in Mark do the companions (associates? relatives?) of Jesus go to restrain him because they thought that he was out of his mind (3:21). We have noticed that in Matthew the process of superhumanizing Jesus has begun; there is no trace of this in Mark. Jesus was not the manifest Messiah in the sense that he stood so far above the mass of humanity that he could not be missed.

On the other hand, it is Mark who says most frequently that the disciples did not perceive, did not understand, did not believe. Commentators do not always notice that Peter's confession that Jesus was the Messiah is followed

almost immediately by an episode which reveals clearly
that Peter has a false idea of secular messiahship (8:27-33).
Most interpreters see in this episode the highpoint or turning point of the Gospel of Mark; it is the turning point in
the sense that here begins the explanation that the messiahship of Jesus was a messiahship of suffering and death.
This, rather than simply the messiahship, was the object
of the messianic secret. This is what the Jews did not believe and what the disciples did not understand; as Mark
related it, they never understood it during the earthly life
of Jesus. The messianic secret in Mark is rather the incredible truth about the Messiah, secret only because human
wisdom and human experience refuse to accept it.

The theological thrust of the Gospel of Mark is not only
to present Jesus Messiah as an object of faith but also to
explain why faith in Jesus Messiah had been denied by so
many who had seen him, and why even his own disciples
did not perceive his reality until after he had left them.
Possibly we do not understand the vividness with which
Mark 14:50 was read or recited in the early churches:
"They all abandoned him and fled." No doubt Peter's denial that Jesus was even known to him was told with the
same vividness (14:66-72). How could such things have
happened? Mark may have been naive, but not so naive as
to explain the dullness and unbelief of the disciples by
saying that Jesus had never told them anything. He had
indeed told them, but he had told them something they
could not believe; and when the suffering Son of Man was
actually killed they simply saw the collapse of the only
Messiahship they had been willing to accept.

The presentation of Jesus Messiah who was the suffering
Son of Man may have a correspondence in the writings of
Paul. Paul often refers to his "gospel," but he never tells in
his letters what it is; when he wrote to churches to which
he had proclaimed his gospel, it was not necessary for him
to repeat it. The letters of Paul show very little interest in
the life of Jesus or in his words. One could hardly deduce

from this that Paul's gospel showed the same degree of interest. This does not imply that Jesus is anything but central in the letters of Paul. Jesus is central because of his saving act as Messiah, because he is the Lord who died for our sins and rose for our righteousness. The emphasis in the letters of Paul is the same as the emphasis in the Gospel of Mark; and some scholars have suggested that the two may have been more closely associated than the New Testament tells us. This conclusion does not seem warranted; the relation between the two is more likely to be that they were both members of the first generation of the church who proclaimed basically the same gospel. It was important that faith be given to Jesus Messiah for what he was, not for what he was not.

Mark is extremely reticent at both the beginning and the end of his Gospel, just the points at which Matthew and Luke have notable expansions. Jesus Messiah first appears at his baptism, and he does not begin to announce the reign until John is silenced by imprisonment. There is nothing about his birth or childhood; and nothing explains this silence except total lack of information. What Jesus was or did before his career was seemingly of no interest. It may be thought that Jesus himself renounced any connection with his antecedent life in such passages as 3:31-35 and 6:1-6, yet Mark gives more details about the strangely unknown kin of Jesus than either Matthew or Luke chose to retain. It is a part of the human portrayal of Jesus. Mark, however, says nothing to suggest that the kinsmen and neighbors of Jesus believed in him at that time or later.

The blank at the end of the Gospel has puzzled interpreters ever since it was recognized that 16:9-20 is missing in the major manuscripts, just the manuscripts on which we depend for any text of the New Testament at all. The same critical evidence which witnesses to the existence of the Gospel of Mark witnesses to the absence of this portion. Close examination of the addition shows that it is a pas-

tiche made up from the resurrection narratives of the other
three Gospels. Critics have argued that the closing sentence, "for they were afraid," is not foreign to Greek style
and does not imply that the last page of the Gospel has
been lost. Yet most interpreters find the ending so abrupt
as to leave a sense of dissatisfaction. The empty tomb is
attested, and an apparition in Galilee is promised but is
never narrated. The "young man" is rather carefully not
called an angel, nor does anything in the angel's speech
suggest that only a heavenly messenger could deliver it.

A mysterious conclusion

The feeling of dissatisfaction arises at least in part from
an implicit comparison with the other three Gospels; yet
the character of the expansions found in these Gospels is
easily recognized by interpreters. They do not come from
Mark, but their theological orientation is not subtle. What
is missing in Mark is the illumination of the disciples which
is affirmed in diverse ways in Matthew, Luke and John.
Mark, the firm witness to the dullness and unbelief of the
disciples, leaves them at the end of his Gospel still dull
and incredulous. An illumination is implicitly promised at
the reunion in Galilee; why does he not relate it? Does he
mean us to conclude that the disciples arrived at faith in
the Risen Messiah and Lord from the events which he has
related here? If he meant this, then he was unaware of the
traditions which Paul mentions in I Corinthians 15:3-7.
And if Mark was a companion of Paul, it can be assumed
that he had at least an opportunity to learn the traditions
which Paul knew. Is it possible that he did not choose to
include them in his Gospel?

It is possible, for the reason that Mark may have understood the Gospel to end with the empty tomb. The Risen
Jesus belongs to a different dimension of reality; that to
Mark may have been another story besides the one which
he had to tell. The experience of the Risen Lord was not

the same as the experience of Jesus Messiah of Nazareth. Mark wrote what he had heard up to the point where another reality is attested. There is hardly any other way to explain the ending which we have. Unless Mark leads into the reality of the Risen Lord, he would hardly have been able to call his book a gospel. He does indeed lead into it, for the proclamation of the suffering Son of Man is the proclamation of one who rises; but for this even Mark cannot give the kind of witness which he gives for the life and death of Jesus of Nazareth.

Chapter Eight

THE GOSPEL OF MARK, CHAPTERS 1–4

Prelude to the Public Ministry of Jesus

Mark alone calls his work "the gospel" [*J. B.* "Good News"] in the *title (1:1)*, and the phrase "the son of God" is missing in the best manuscripts. Mark has no infancy narrative and no genealogy, but begins at once with *the preaching of John the Baptist (1:2-8)*, whom Mark identifies with the messenger of Malachi 3:1 and the voice of Isaiah 40:3. John proclaimed repentance, externalized by a confession of sin and a symbolic bathing. He announces the coming of "a mightier one" whose baptism will be more than symbolic; but the early church did distinguish ritually between baptism and the conferring of the Holy Spirit (Acts 8:14-19; 19:1-7). The "mightier one" appears immediately in *the baptism of Jesus (1:9-11)*; it is clear in Mark's version that the vision and the voice were perceived only by Jesus. *The temptation of Jesus (1:12-13)* is told in a much shorter form than in Matthew and Luke, who have expanded the story from another source; the mere fact of the temptation of Jesus must have been scandalous to some, and thus Matthew and Luke apparently thought it was necessary to specify. Mark indicates an attack of evil spirits upon Jesus after he is manifested as "the beloved son." Mark's narrative does not suggest the new Moses and the new Israel, but rather a new Adam, at peace with all the wild animals and served by angels.

A summary of the preaching of Jesus (1:14-15) is typical of Mark, who often reports that Jesus taught but does not tell us the contents of the preaching or the teaching. Here the content is the announcement of the arrival of the reign of God, and the imperative is to believe the "good news" (gospel); for the arrival of the reign is good news, the coming of the climactic saving act of God.

The call of the first disciples (1:16-20) was addressed to the two pairs of brothers, Simon-Andrew and James-John, all fishermen, and hence chosen to be "fishers of men"; the saying may reflect the actual experience of apostleship. The point of the story is no doubt the immediate obedience to the call and the renunciation of family and occupation.

The account of *a day in Capernaum (1:21-34)* is intended to relate a typical day in the ministry of Jesus. The first miracle reported by Mark is the *exorcism of a demoniac (1:21-28).* This shows that the authority of his teaching (1:22) is backed by an unparalleled power. In Jesus, God begins the campaign which will drive the power of Satan out of the world. The devils recognize the arrival of the new power, even though the Jews do not. The *cure of the mother-in-law of Simon (1:29-31)* is reported for its instantaneous effect; she rose and prepared supper for the several guests. *A number of cures (1:32-34)* are effected in the last hour of daylight, too numerous to specify; in this typical "day" Mark has made the healing power of Jesus so routine that only the notable cures are worth individual mention. *The departure from Capernaum (1:35-39)* is preceded by a long prayer; Jesus' praying, while it is not mentioned often, must have had a quality which the disciples observed in no other person. The departure, described in a foreshortened perspective like the day in Capernaum, introduces the wide scope of the mission of Jesus on the second day of the mission. *The cure of the leper (1:40-45)* makes its point by the verbal echo of the petition (1:40) in the cure (1:41). For the first time Mark introduces his theme of "the messianic secret" in 1:44; Jesus did not wish his messiahship to be prematurely announced, but the power he exhibited could not be con-

cealed. Manifest power is a far more convincing demonstration than verbal affirmation.

Controversy with the Scribes

The theme of controversy with the scribes, which runs
through all of the Gospels, is introduced in *the cure of the
paralytic (2:1-12)*. The story evinces the growth of faith in
the power of Jesus, but moves from his power to heal
disease to his power to heal sin, the cause of disease. This
was not a messianic power but a definition of the true
nature of messianic power and of the saving act of God
which Jesus announced. If the paralytic was a typical case,
he was much more concerned about the cure of his disease
than he was about the forgiveness of his sins. Jesus re-
establishes the priorities. *The call of Levi (2:13-14)*, like
the call of the first four disciples, is an instance of another
power of Jesus, the power to summon men to an instantaneous and total response.

The story about the dinner (2:15-17) is a "saying-story."
When Jesus was charged with a liking for low company, he
did not disclaim the charge but observed that they needed
him. Implicit is the charge that he cannot speak to those
who do not recognize their need. *The discussion about
fasting (2:18-22)* implies that Jesus did not follow the
rabbinical fasting customs; these were what we call "de-
votional practices," not of obligation, but expected of one
who professed great devotion to the Law. Jesus did not
profess such devotion. The answer equivalently means
that one does not fast when one has heard "good news"
(1:15). It is all but certain that 2:20 was written in view of
the adoption of fasting by early Christians; the saying
about fasting is set in a context which affirms the novelty
of the Christian event, and this novelty is not to be
affirmed by the retention of Jewish practices. *The discussion on Sabbath observance (2:23-28)* is set off by the
opposition between a human need, even if the need was

less than vital, and the rigorous Pharisaic Sabbath observance. The problem is solved by an appeal to Scripture, and
two sayings (2:27) are appended; the second saying is not
used by Matthew and Luke, possibly because it was regarded as too bold to be easily understood. The saying
can mean "Man" (and not the Son of Man, Jesus) is lord
of the Sabbath; this does indeed follow more easily from
the first saying, and is so radical that it can be attributed
to no one but Jesus. The early church very probably understood the saying as an assertion of authority by Jesus.

The theme of the Sabbath observance is again brought
up in *the story of the cure of the withered hand (3:1-6).*
The question very probably identifies doing evil and kill-
ing (3:4) with the attitude of the Pharisees; to refuse help
on the Sabbath is to do harm and even to kill, not positively but by deliberate refusal to act.

A summary of miracles (3:7-12) contrasts the plotting of
the Pharisees (3:6) with the reception of Jesus by the
people; the theme of the messianic secret is repeated (3:11-
12). *The choice of the Twelve (3:13-19)* serves to give a
complete list of those who were to share the company of
Jesus and his mission; and all the Gospels identify the one
who was faithless.

The story about Jesus and his family (3:20-21) is found
only in Mark; without doubt Matthew and Luke found this
too difficult to repeat. If the story is continued at 3:31,
which is very probable, then "his relatives" are more
specifically identified there. Commentators have always
noted that the presence of the mother of Jesus does not
indicate that she shared the relatives' sentiments. The
belief that Jesus cherished delusions of grandeur is quite
in harmony with the account of the visit of Jesus to Nazareth (6:1-6) and informs us that the rejection was not
limited to neighbors and acquaintances.

The Beelzebub controversy (3:22-30), following immediately upon the notice of the relatives of Jesus and
possibly even interrupting the narrative, seems intended

to associate the unbelief of the relatives of Jesus with the unbelief of the Pharisees. The charge of being in league with the devil scarcely admitted a biblical refutation. If Jesus expels devils through Beelzebub, then the reign of the devil has already collapsed through internal strife. This argument is indeed logical, but it scarcely refutes the charge that Jesus is in league with the devil. This is stated more clearly in 3:27. The kingdom of Satan, one can judge from its power, must be a strong centralized monarchy; this was the most powerful type of government known in the ancient world. Such a power can be mastered only by conquering the central seat of power. The severity of 3:29 is an ancient exegetical and theological problem; the verse can mean only that refusal to recognize the works of the spirit is refusal to recognize God by the only means available. A permanent denial of God is within man's reach, and the identification of God with the devil is perilously close to a permanent denial.

At this juncture Mark reintroduces the relatives of Jesus; after the scribes have declared that he is in league with the devil, his relatives appear with the conviction that he is crazy. It is against this background that the severity of *the saying about the kinsmen of Jesus (3:31-35)* must be understood. Commentators have been excessively annoyed by the reference to the mother of Jesus. In the typical Palestinian village most of the residents are related by blood or by marriage or by both to most of the other residents. Unbelief severs the relation of kinship, the closest relationship known in the whole of the Jewish world. Faith in Jesus founds a new community of a new type, community of the believers with Jesus and with each other.

The Parable Discourse

Only in *the parable discourse (4:1-35)*, and later in the eschatological discourse (13:1-37) does Mark present the teaching of Jesus at length. The discourse is addressed to

the public only as far as 4:9; the rest of the chapter is
addressed to the disciples. Of the three parables only the
first (the sower) is given at length, and only the first is interpreted. *The parable of the sower (4:1-9)* without the
interpretation given in 4:13-20 would most easily be interpreted to mean that the reign proclaimed by Jesus will
surely come in spite of obstacles, as the harvest infallibly
arrives in spite of obstacles which are never overcome. *A
saying about parables (4:10-12)* is inserted between the
parable of the sower and its interpretation. The saying in
Mark is extremely harsh, more so than in Matthew and
Luke. Without doubt some of the harshness is due to the
poverty of Hebrew grammar, which had no syntactical
distinction between purpose and result; and this difficulty
is found not only in Mark, but in the text of Isaiah 6:9-10,
quoted here, and in several other passages of the Old
Testament. But this is only part of the difficulty. It was a
biblical belief that nothing happened apart from God's
intention; and this theological problem is genuine for
Christians as well as for ancient Israelites. Parables were
used by the rabbis as a pedagogical technique, in the belief
that the student's interest was heightened and his skill
sharpened by compelling him to penetrate through deliberately obscure sayings. The "mystery" of the reign is
not merely an obscure saying but an entirely new reality;
and thus any expression of the reign would be a "riddle,"
since the language of experience is not adequate to express it. The parable leads the listener to inquire in simple
faith for the explanation which is given the disciples; "the
others" refuse to ask because of ingrained prejudice and
the conviction that God will perform no new act.

The explanation of the parable of the sower (4:13-20) is
regarded by commentators as an explanation of the early
church and not of Jesus. Allegory is thought to be foreign
to the teaching of Jesus, as it was foreign to rabbinical
methods. The church found a new level of meaning in the
parable as a recital of the obstacles to faith. The parable

is followed by two sayings which illustrate very clearly the principle of the catchword. *The saying about the lamp (4:21-23)* echoes the idea of concealment (4:10-12), and thus supports the theory that the explanation of the parable is an insertion. It should be noticed that the prohibition of concealing the light must be considered as a part of the solution of the problem of the harsh saying about parables; Jesus did not intend the parables to be the bushel under which his own light was hidden. *The saying about the measure (4:24-25)* echoes the word *modion* (4:21, translated "tub," a vessel of a determined size). The two parts of 4:24-25 are divided in Matthew (Mt. 7:2 refers to justice in dealing with others, and Mt. 25:29 refers to the reward for the proper use of the talents.) It appears that these sayings were fragmented and taken out of their original contexts before they were compiled in Mark.

The parable of the seed (4:26-29), found only in Mark, like the parable of the sower, expresses the certainty of the coming of the reign, and adds the note that the work of God, which cannot be observed, brings the reign to pass.

The parable of the mustard seed (4:30-32) contrasts the humble, even unseen origins of the reign with its fullness. This can hardly reflect the experience of the church, and it is with good reason taken as one of the expressions of the universal scope of the reign which can be attributed to Jesus himself. The *conclusion (4:33-34)* repeats the same pattern of thought which is found in 4:10-12.

The three parables are followed by three miracles; the first is *the calming of the storm (4:35-41)*. Mark's storm is less cosmic than Matthew's version, and Mark alone has the vivid detail of Jesus napping on a cushion in the stern while the boat takes on water in large quantities. Mark also has the direct words of Jesus, which contain a rather earthy version of the English "Shut up!" The question of the disciples (4:41) strangely ignores the earlier recognition given Jesus by demons, and in its original context was very probably not associated with this recognition.

Chapter Nine

THE GOSPEL OF
MARK, CHAPTERS 5–8

The Miracles of Jesus

The episode of *the Gerasene demoniac (5:1-20)* is an excellent illustration of Mark's wealth of detail in narrative, much of which is omitted by Matthew and Luke. The interest of the original story was certainly in its location outside of Jewish territory and the exorcism of a Gentile; Mark's readers and hearers would have been less troubled by demonic possession and the destruction of the herd of swine than modern readers are. The original story of the cure has certainly been largely fictionalized; unexplained illnesses, especially mental illness, were normally attributed to demonic or some supernatural influence, but this hardly explains the pigs. One should seek some theological significance in the embellishment; and the story obviously signifies that the word of Jesus spoken in Gentile territory does indeed liberate men from the power of Satan but at the cost of damage in material goods. The response of the Gentiles is not hostile unbelief like the response of the scribes, but a simple request that this frighteningly powerful man should leave their territory. The conclusion indicates that Jesus himself intended to make no disciples among the Gentiles, but that his works could be proclaimed; Mark reflects the ambiguity of the primitive church in its attitude towards the Gentiles.

The raising of the daughter of Jairus (5:21-43) is again narrated with more detail than Matthew and Luke have retained. It is not clear whether the words of Jesus (5:39)

signify apparent or real death; Matthew, and very probably Luke, understood them to mean real death. This is the
first episode in which Peter, James and John were selected
to witness an event; these were three of the first four
chosen (1:16-20), and one wonders why Andrew was ex-
cluded. The raising in any case shows that faith in Jesus
the healer ceased when death, real or apparent, super-
vened; and the petitioner must not fear but believe (5:36).

Within the story of the raising of Jairus' daughter is the
healing of the woman with a hemorrhage. Matthew has
omitted and Luke softened the inquiry of Jesus as to who
touched him (5:30-33; see Matthew 9:20-22 and Luke 8:43-
48). It was difficult to understand how Jesus could heal
without knowing who was being healed or even of what
the person had been healed, but could only sense that the
power of his person had accomplished something. That
Jesus was a person of power is abundantly clear, but the
idea of his personal power implicit in this narrative is
naive. This personal power is activated for the petitioner
by faith even without an express petition, and this distinguishes the naive idea of a personal power from magic.

The account of the *rejection at Nazareth (6:1-6)* must be
considered with the previous references to the relatives of
Jesus (3:20-21, 31-35). Distinguished guests were invited
to speak in synagogues which they visited; plainly the
people of Nazareth would not accept Jesus as a distinguished guest. And in Mark there is no indication that
what Jesus said was offensive, as Luke's expanded version of the incident suggests (4:16-30). The episode is a
"saying-story" with its climax in 6:4. Mark's version of
the saying not only clearly refers to the relatives of Jesus
but seems to move from outer to inner circles: country,
relatives, house. Miracles clearly depend on faith in 6:5;
Matthew changed "could not" to "did not" and made the
statement less difficult. The saying could have been directed at Palestinian Judaism rather than at Nazareth, and
the implications of the saying are certainly wider than
Nazareth.

The account of *the mission of the Twelve (6:7-13)* contains instructions which are closely retained by Matthew
and Luke. In comparison with Matthew, Mark forbids
bread but permits staff and sandals; and Mark's version is
realistic, while Matthew and Luke turn the instructions
into a more idealized precept of evangelical poverty. The
symbolic gesture of shaking dust from one's feet indicates
unclean territory; the unbelieving Jew is reduced to the
status of the pagan.

The *opinions about Jesus (6:14-16)* anticipate the answer
of the disciples in 8:28. Both the risen John the Baptist and
Elijah identify Jesus with "the eschatological prophet," the
last prophet who will announce the coming of the Messiah;
a prophet "like one of the prophets" seems to deny this
identification, although it was normal in this period of
Judaism to believe that the succession of prophets had
ended. The opinion of Herod, if it is quoted accurately,
could have expressed either ironical unbelief or superstitious fear; and it gives Mark an occasion to add as an appendix the episode which follows.

The Death of John the Baptist

The death of John the Baptist (6:17-29) again exhibits a
fullness of detail not found in Matthew; Luke omitted the
passage, very probably because he found it entirely unedi-
fying. The Jewish historian Josephus also reported the
incident but did not mention John's rebuke of Herod's
adultery. From Josephus come the place of the execution,
Machaerus, and the name of the daughter of Herodias,
Salome. In spite of the rather romantic nature of the narrative and the fact that it must have come from popular
legend, few have questioned its historical character. The
influence of John upon Herod, attested by Mark and by
Josephus, may be an instance of the superstitious fear
mentioned in connection with 6:14-15; Herod Antipas
seems to have been an entirely irreligious man.

The feeding of the five thousand (6:30-44) follows the
return of the Twelve; the time elapsed is not indicated.

Only Mark connects the journey to an uninhabited region (not the desert proper) with the invitation to rest after the journey. The place is not further identified, but on the basis of 6:32 and 6:45 it could not have been far from the Sea of Galilee. Mark again is fuller in details, and his dialogue between Jesus and the disciples shows clearly the ironical response of the disciples to the suggestion of Jesus that they provide food for the crowd; the narrator creates suspense. The scene and the details of the wonder are full of allusions to the past and the present works of God. The "desert" reminds the hearer of the manna which Israel ate in the desert (Exodus 16:12-35). The words which describe the actions of Jesus (6:41) anticipate the institution of the Eucharist (14:22). The division of the crowd into companies of one hundred and of fifty not only echoes the organization of the Israelites (Exodus 18:25) but also the arrangements for the messianic banquet, as described in the literature of Qumran. And while it may be far fetched, some have seen in "the green grass" of 6:39, together with "sheep without a shepherd" (6:34; see 1 Kings 22:17), an allusion to Psalm 23:1-5. The episode is clearly an anticipation both of the Eucharist and of the eschatological messianic banquet (Isaiah 25:6). The allusions to this wonder are more frequent and clearer than allusions to any other miracle attributed to Jesus; and these allusions scarcely justify interpreting the event as entirely symbolic, although the construction of the narrative is clearly heavy with symbolic details. The event is as important for its theological significance as for its historical reality.

Jesus walks on Water

The walking on the sea (6:45-52) does answer a question implicit in the narrative: How did Jesus rejoin the disciples? Only John 6:15 gives misguided messianic fervor as the reason for the sudden dismissal both of the disciples and of the crowd. Yet the symbolism of the narrative is transparent; the disciples alone at sea in the storm repre-

sent the church, and Jesus is never far from the church,
even when his presence cannot be discerned. That the
disciples did not understand "concerning the loaves" (6:52)
was so puzzling to Matthew that he omitted it (as Luke
omitted the entire pericope of the walking on the water),
and it is not much less puzzling to modern commentators.
If the symbolism of the narrative has been correctly interpreted, Mark means that the disciples did not see in the
miracle of the loaves a messianic sign. The sequence closes
with a summary of miracles (6:53-56); the details mentioned echo miracle stories given elsewhere in Mark.

The *dispute about uncleanness (7:1-23)* is compiled from
various sayings of Jesus which deal generally with the
same topic. Jesus first speaks to the Pharisees, then to the
crowd, then to the disciples. Mark explains for his Gentile
readers the Jewish practice or ritual ablutions (7:3-4). This
type of ritual ablution, originally intended to preserve the
ritual cleanliness of the priests, was extended by "the
tradition of the elders" (7:3, 5) to all who desired to observe the Law fully and exactly. The answer of Jesus is
more severe than might be expected. The first answer, the
quotation of Isaiah 29:13, does not answer the question of
cleanliness directly, but opposes the commandments of
God to their own traditions (7:6-9). In Pharisaic Judaism
the traditions had the same value as the Law; Jesus denies
this. The next step in the answer illustrates the evasion of
the commandment of honoring the parents by the device
of donating one's goods to the temple; one could use the
revenues of the goods for oneself but not for profane
purposes. Yet the commandment to honor one's parents
was understood to include supporting them in their old
age. The question of cleanliness is then dealt with by the
saying in 7:14-15, put in the riddle form of a wise saying,
which effectively denies the principle of ritual cleanliness.
Jesus is impatient with the emphasis on external and symbolic cleanliness combined with the neglect of interior
cleanliness. The only "unclean" object in all creation is

man himself, who produces the uncleanness of moral vice. Possibly there is an implicit criticism of the snobbishness of the Pharisees; one who attempted to observe the ritual ablutions could hardly afford either to engage in manual labor or to associate with people who were not as clean as himself.

The cure of the daughter of the Syro-Phoenician woman (7:24-30) is one of the rare encounters of Jesus with Gentiles; and the designation of the woman as Syro-Phoenician, not found elsewhere, is puzzling. The saying of Jesus (7:27) is harsh, and Matthew has somewhat softened it by an expansion (15:24) which makes explicit the refusal of Jesus to extend his ministry to Gentiles; this is no doubt the meaning of the saying in Mark. But the saying would have been less harsh where it was uttered; and the exchange is an excellent example of "wisdom," which was often an exchange of wit. The woman caps Jesus' wise saying, turns it to her advantage, and is rewarded "for saying this" (7:29). Mark understood the dialogue better than Matthew, who made the miracle a reward of faith (15:28). *The healing of the deaf mute (7:31-37)* was omitted by both Matthew and Luke, very probably because it has some singular features; the use of touch and spittle, the sigh or groan, and the direct address, although no demonic possession is mentioned, have no parallel. One asks whether this procedure occurred more frequently and happens to be mentioned only here. The Gospels show a developing idea of the transcendence of the power of Jesus. Both here and in 5:30 Mark preserves a more primitive idea of the power of Jesus.

The feeding of the four thousand (8:1-10) must be a parallel version of the feeding of the five thousand. Mark could not merge them, and he placed this in Gentile territory (the Decapolis, 7:31), making it an anticipation of the messianic banquet for the Gentiles as the first feeding was such an anticipation for the Jews.

The refusal of a sign (8:11-13) was expanded by Matthew

and Luke, who probably found the simple refusal of a sign too difficult. The meaning of the sign can be understood somewhat from Isaiah 7:10-11 as any wonder in the visible universe. The response of Jesus says that he has given them enough of a sign. In this context the response of Jesus to the disciples in the discussion of *the yeast of the Pharisees (8:14-21)* loses none of its severity but becomes more intelligible. In a rapid series of seven questions the disciples' blindness (stupidity is a better word) is reduced to a moral level not far above the unbelief of the Pharisees. Such stupidity can scarcely be involuntary; and it is most likely that the "yeast" is the refusal to accept the true nature of the messiahship of Jesus, a refusal which the disciples shared. Unlike Matthew, Mark leaves the saying unexplained—and the disciples presumably still without understanding.

This severe rebuke is a prelude to the great reversal which follows, the turning point in the Gospel of Mark, the confession of Peter. It is no doubt the theme of blindness gradually cured which led Mark to insert here *the cure of the blind man of Bethsaida (8:22-26)*. The cure is gradual, and spittle and dirt are employed; again, these singular features are the reasons why Matthew and Luke did not employ this episode. The man who at first sees only dimly and then sees fully suggests Peter in the following episode.

The confession of Peter and the first prediction of the passion (8:27-33) were anticipated by the opinions about Jesus recited in 6:14-16. Matthew has enlarged the episode; in Mark it is a simple recognition of the messiahship of Jesus. Peter is not expressly said to speak for the group, but the implication is clear. That Peter did not know what messiahship meant is clear from his response to the prediction of the passion, a response which is rebuked by Jesus with utmost severity. Peter's refusal to accept a suffering messiah was "the yeast of the Pharisees." By verbal association the prediction of the passion is followed by *sayings about discipleship (8:34-9:1)*. The disciple of the suffering Messiah must accept suffering, even the cross and death, in maintaining his profession of faith. Only by losing his "self" or his "life" (the Greek word is ambiguous) can he save his "self" or his "life" in the world to come. The saying of 9:1 is eschatological, attracted to this context by the "glory" in 8:38; its interpretation follows the principles applied to the eschatological discourse (13:1-37).

Chapter Ten

THE GOSPEL OF
MARK, CHAPTERS 9–12

The Transfiguration

The transfiguration (9:2-8) is best understood as the experience of a vision, with its description enlarged by the use of symbolism. Jesus is seen as the fulfillment of the Old Testament which is signified by Moses (the Law) and Elijah (the prophets). But the consummation of the messiahship of Jesus is not yet reached; the disciples may not yet enter into repose. By verbal association *the question concerning Elijah (9:9-13)* follows. In Judaism Elijah was expected to return as the precursor of the Messiah; Jesus identifies John the Baptist as the returning Elijah.

The cure of the demoniac (9:14-29) is presented as a test of faith. The victory of Jesus over demonic power is conditioned by the faith of those for whom the victory is achieved. The symptoms of the child are recognized as the symptoms of epilepsy. In the primitive medicine of New Testament times these symptoms were attributed to demonic possession, and this popular belief is accepted in the narrative without criticism. *The second prediction of the passion (9:30-32)* is a repetition of the first (8:31-33); the disciples do not understand the prediction, although nothing like the gross misunderstanding of Peter (8:32-33) is reported in this context.

The dispute about greatness (9:33-37) is resolved by a saying which actually looks two ways and hence has probably been extended from its original context; the disciples are told to be like little children and to receive little chil-

93

dren. The connection seems to be purely verbal. The saying about receiving little children is nearly a doublet of
10:13-16; the saying about greatness is parallel to 10:41-45.
A collection of sayings (9:38-50) is attached here by verbal
association ("disciples" and "little ones"). The saying of
9:40, compared with its antitheses in Matthew 12:30 and
Luke 11:23 (no parallel in Mark), becomes a Christian
paradox; each version of the saying must be taken in its
own context. The saying about the cup of water (9:41) is
appended here by the catchword "name." The sayings on
scandal (9:42-50) are rigorous; hyperbole is used, but the
renunciation demanded by the reign must not be minimized. The saying about salt and fire is added by verbal
association. Salt is here a means of purification.

   The question about divorce (10:1-12) is not put in the
rabbinical form (see Matthew 19:1-9). Mark's version of
the saying cannot be original, for it is addressed to Roman
law, in which the wife was permitted to divorce her husband; in Jewish law only the husband could divorce.
Mark's saying thus becomes more rigorous than the saying
in Matthew. *The blessing of the children (10:13-16)* is accomplished against the wishes of the disciples; only Mark
records the indignation of Jesus. The disposition of the
child, which in 9:35 is required of one who would be first
among the disciples, is here required as a condition of
simple entrance into the reign. *Mark's story of the rich
young man (10:17-23)* contains a saying about the goodness
of God alone which was too harsh for both Matthew and
Luke. Only Mark reports that Jesus loved the questioner.
The recommendation to keep the commandments is
equivalently a recommendation to be an observant Jew;
one who wishes more is invited to become a disciple. *The
saying about riches (10:23-27)* clearly indicates that wealth
is an obstacle to discipleship. What God makes possible
is the renunciation of wealth; it is not implied that this
renunciation need be done at a single stroke. *The reward of
renunciation (10:28-31)* is sufficiency for one's needs and

life eternal; it is no doubt implied that one who renounces
all his goods will share in the common possessions of the
Christian community, which will not allow its members to
suffer privation. The third prediction of the passion (10:32-
34) is more explicit than the first (8:31-33) and the second
(9:30-32); the details reflect the event.

Authority in the Kingdom of God

The request of the sons of Zebedee (10:35-40) follows
the prediction of the passion by topical association; it is a
striking instance of the failure of the disciples to grasp the
mystery of the suffering Messiah. That Jesus denies his
power to assign seats is a difficult saying, preserved in
spite of its difficulty. Such sayings do not permit a facile
statement of the relations between Jesus and the Father.
The request is the occasion of the saying about authority
(10:41-45); Jesus clearly rejects any structure of authority
in his community which is modeled after political authority. Jesus himself serves others by dying on their behalf,
and those who bear authority in his name must conduct
themselves as the lackeys of their fellow believers. The
journey to Jerusalem approaches its end at Jericho with
the cure of the blind man (10:46-52). The blind man invokes
Jesus by the messianic title of "son of David," but there is
no longer any effort to keep the messianic secret; the
Messiah reveals himself in the following passage.

Although Mark does not allude to the text, the entrance
of Jesus into Jerusalem (11:1-11) is such a clear echo of
Zechariah 9:9 that hardly any interpreter doubts that a
reenactment was deliberately intended. The Messiah king
appears as meek and lowly, riding upon an ass, without the
trappings of royalty and the panoply of war; he is the very
antithesis of the conquering political and military hero.
The curse of the fig tree (11:12-14) is commonly understood
as a parabolic saying of Jesus which early tradition transformed into an event (11:20). The fig tree symbolizes

Pharisaic Judaism, which had all the appearances of piety
without any of the genuine works of piety. In *the cleansing
of the temple (11:15-19)* Jesus removes from the temple
any commercial activity as incompatible with the place of
prayer—a rigor which has not always been imitated by
Christians. Mark's interest in Gentiles seems to be reflected
in his quotation of Isaiah 56:7 in full ("for all peoples");
the commercial transactions were conducted in the Court
of the Gentiles.

Sayings about Faith

Sayings about faith (11:20-25) are attached to the episode of the cursing of the fig tree (see above). It is a con-
stant evangelical theme, found in a number of miracle
stories, that miracles are possible only with faith; they do
not depend purely on the power of God. The saying about
the faith which moves mountains was proverbial as early
as 1 Corinthians 13:2. The saying of 11:25 echoes the
Lord's Prayer (Matthew 6:14), a prayer doubtless known
to Mark and his community even though Mark does not
give the prayer. Mark 11:26 is derived from Matthew 6:15,
and does not belong to the critical text of Mark.

The question of the authority of Jesus (11:27-33) is
evaded rather than answered; but the question of Jesus
about the authority of John is altogether legitimate. By
failing to answer this question the priests and scribes
effectively disqualify themselves from investigating the
authority of Jesus. It was their business to discern the
quality of religious leadership and teaching, and they confess their failure to do this in a very important case. It
should be noticed that Jesus implicitly rejects the religious
authority of the Jewish leaders; and the dialogue makes it
clear that he rejects their authority because their use of
authority is governed by personal interest.

The parable of the wicked husbandmen (12:1-12) is one
of the few parables of Mark; and this parable raises a
question as to whether it is a parable of Jesus himself or

an early Christian interpretation of the rejection of Jesus
by the Jews. In its present form the parable seems to be an
expansion of a saying of Jesus. It is not clear that the total
rejection of Jesus, which is implied in the parable but did
not become a reality until later in the first century, was
ever anticipated in the words of Jesus himself. The parable
is based on land laws of Palestine of the time. If the heirs
of an absentee landlord failed to appear to assert their claim
to the property, the land passed to the tenant farmers.

The question of the tribute to Caesar (12:13-17) is almost
the only saying of Jesus which has any direct bearing on
politics. The question, like some others, is evaded rather
than answered; Jesus does not define what belongs to
Caesar and what belongs to God, and this decision seems
to be imposed upon the Christian conscience within the
Christian community. If there is a simple rule, it is not
given here. The answer reminds the inquirers that the use
of Caesar's money is a tacit acknowledgement of the
sovereignty of Caesar; thus they have already answered in
practice their own question about the legitimacy of Caesar.

The Ressurection of the Dead

The question of the resurrection (12:18-27) is a typical
example of ingenious rabbinical discussion; and the answer of Jesus meets the question with the same rabbinical
ingenuity. Jesus clearly says that marriage belongs to this
life and is terminated by death. The Sadducees, who accepted only the Law of Moses as scripture, had to be answered with a quotation from the Law. The argument rests
on grammar rather than on content, and takes advantage
of the position of the questioners; the Sadducees could not
admit that God was God of the dead.

The question about the greatest commandment (12:28-34)
is not given in the rabbinical form in which Matthew gives
it—probably closer to the original form. The rabbis discussed "heavy" and "light" commandments in order to
solve problems of conflicting obligations. Jesus cites two

commandments as the heaviest of all; Matthew and Paul state more clearly that these two are as heavy as all the others, 611 in number. Mark's favorable presentation of the scribe is peculiar to himself, although Luke (10:25-28) makes the scribe himself recite the two commandments. Matthew represents the inquirer as hostile.

The question of the son of David (12:35-37) is another example of rabbinical virtuosity, and it is a mistake to think of Jesus as "teaching" anything in this example. He simply presents the experts with an exegetical riddle which depends for its meaning on a play on words; the purpose is not to teach but to discredit the teachers of Judaism. *The saying about the scribes (12:38-40)* is only a fragment compared to the speech found in Matthew 23. Mark condemns the scribes for hypocrisy and avarice; actually this verse has no parallel in Matthew, and Mark has no parallel elsewhere to Matthew's invective. Mark 12:40 came into many manuscripts of Matthew as 23:14.

The widow's mite (12:41-44) contains a saying on almsgiving which evaluates the gift in terms of loss to the giver and not in its absolute quantity. Almsgiving was a duty often proclaimed in Judaism, and the early church preserved sayings in which Jesus also proclaimed this duty. This saying makes it clear that if almsgiving does not hurt, it is not a virtue.

Reflections on Mark

We observed in the introduction to Mark that the second Gospel has fewer sayings of Jesus than the other Gospels. The section identified as Part III is the richest of the sections in sayings, and it can be rewarding to find the emphasis if we can; for this section may represent the earliest memories of what Jesus said. We cannot recover his "exact words," which so many people desire; but we may put some confidence in the report of the major themes and emphases.

A glance at the headings shows that the major themes are power and authority, both civil and religious, and the poor and helpless. In Palestine of the first century of our era the political power was held by a foreign government. But that type of power which touched most frequently and most closely the lives of most of the people was the power based on wealth. The power structure of wealth did not capture or employ the power of the state, but it preserved itself by cooperation with the political power.

Distinct both from political power and the power of wealth was the power of the religious leaders of Judaism. This power was the influence which comes from recognized conformity to generally accepted standards and from the knowledge which enabled the leaders to interpret these standards for the majority of the people who accepted them.

Apart from the relations of wealth to political power, which were common in countries governed by foreign powers, relations in Palestine at the time of Jesus were not radically different from the relations which the modern American knows in his own society. There is no historical foundation for affirming that either the political power, the economic power or the religious power were in the hands of entirely corrupt men. To imply that Jesus encountered totally corrupt power permits one to say that his words are not applicable to our own situation. And many prefer not to apply them, because the attitude of Jesus towards the three types of power mentioned is distinctly cool.

The relations of the Jews with the Roman government were complex and elicited several different answers, maintained by different groups with bitter hostility. For this most urgent political question of his own people Jesus had no time and no answer. What he offers men is indifferent to the type of government under which they live; they can accept his message under any government. Conversely, no government helps men to achieve what his message promises. Not since Constantine established the church legally has the church as a whole been able to live with the utterly non-political attitude of Jesus to civil government. He treated it as simply unimportant.

Mark has less emphasis on poverty than Luke has, but only because the number of texts is smaller. The renunciation is as total as it is in Luke. Wealth is not, like civil government, indifferent to the message of Jesus; it is hostile to the message. The authors of the Gospels knew that these sayings were harsh. The plea of Christians that they can do so much good with wealth is implicitly answered by the suggestion that the good they ought to do will impoverish them. One may argue, as many have argued, that Jesus uses hyperbole here; his language is not saved by dealing with the problems of wealth and poverty as if he had said nothing on the subject. At the very least behind the hyperbole is a kind of sharing of wealth which the Christian community as a whole has never achieved. Nor has the Christian community clearly seen that one need not have wealth to be attached to it.

When Jesus spoke to the religious authorities of Judaism he had in no way set himself up as an opposite authority, a kind of Jewish Reformer. In the words of Matthew, the authorities sat in the chair of Moses. Ultimately Jesus said that they were unfaithful to their responsibilities, but he said it in much more colorful language, as if he did not want the point to be lost in abstractions. Furthermore, in this section he appears as ridiculing them precisely in their area of claimed competence, the area of learning. He asks them trick questions which they are unable to answer. In modern terms he undermines the confidence which people place in them. Since we have observed that they could not be called entirely corrupt, we may ask what their basic vice was; and it turns out that it was the defense of the status quo. They believed that they had carried Judaism as far as it would go. There was nothing for them to learn which they did not know, nothing for them to do which they had not done. Any one who attempted to move them beyond where they stood attacked the most ancient and the most sacred institutions of Judaism, institutions which had been given them by Yahweh himself.

To these claims Jesus showed neither due respect nor due obedience, nor did he spare the persons who held authority. One can remark only that in Christian tradition Jesus criticized religious authority so well and so finally that he left no room for Christians ever to do it again.

Chapter Eleven

THE GOSPEL OF MARK, CHAPTERS 13–16

The Eschatological Discourse

The eschatological discourse (13:1-37) is best understood as a composition of Mark, or possibly of one of his sources. The discourse is based on collected sayings of Jesus, expanded and adapted to answer questions about the last days. Apocalyptic eschatology (which deals with the end of the world) appeared in Judaism; it was an expression of hope in times of persecution and affirmed the coming of God to judge persecutors and to deliver the faithful. Not all the elements of the discourse are apocalyptic. Jesus announced *the destruction of the temple (13:1-2),* which is announced as a historical event. A common feature of apocalyptic literature was *the "sign" by which the arrival of the end-time could be discerned (13:3-4).* The answer of Jesus enumerates *events which are typical of apocalyptic literature (13:5-8);* these do not indicate the end, but rather the beginning of the disasters called in apocalyptic literature "the birthpangs of the Messiah" (13:8). *The warning against persecutions (13:9-13;* see Matthew 10:13-22 and Luke 12:11-12) is not eschatological, and probably reflects the experience of the early church; but the announcement that the gospel must be proclaimed to the world (13:10) is taken as an implicit allusion to the end of the world.

The tribulation of Jerusalem (13:14-20) likewise has no eschatological content; it is the prediction of a historical disaster, which early Christians saw fulfilled in the destruction of the city and the temple in 70 A.D. Mark, as

compared with Matthew and Luke, appears to have been
written before the event. The "abomination" (13:14) is a
reference to Daniel 9:27, which in turn refers to Antiochus
IV Epiphanes, the Seleucid king. It is impossible to find
any concrete reference in the period of the New Testament,
and the allusion speaks generally of the profanation and
destruction of the temple. *The warning against false Mes-
siahs (13:21-23)* has no clear historical reference, and is to
be related to the eschatological period; pretenders will appear before *the real coming of the Son of Man (13:24-27).*
This is the cosmic event, the end of the world; the imagery
is derived from Daniel 7:13-14, and the same imagery appears in 14:62. *The signs of the event (13:28-30)* remain too
vague for precision; to what do "these things" (28-29) refer? Any precise statement is nullified by 13:32, where
Jesus denies exact knowledge even to the Son. One must
take this statement seriously as not invented by primitive
Christians and adjust one's theories about the knowledge
of Jesus accordingly. *The final warning to perpetual vigilance (13:33-37)* likewise suggests no revelation of the time
of the coming of the Son of Man.

 The conspiracy against Jesus (14:1-2, 10-11) has been
split into two sections; the opportunity sought by the
chief priests and the scribes is independently offered by
Judas. Mark gives no motives either for the conspiracy of
the Jewish leaders or for the treachery of Judas; for the
leaders it was the threat which Jesus placed to their authority, for Judas disappointment at a non-political Messiah. The conspiracy story is interrupted by *the anointing
at Bethany (14:3-9).* The saying is certainly intended neither to patronize poverty nor to disdain almsgiving; rather
Jesus points out that the extravagance which the woman
directs towards his person is not matched by the extravagance of those who praise almsgiving but do it in mod-
eration. *The preparation for the Passover (14:12-16)* in
Mark's version contains nothing incompatible with previous arrangements unknown to the disciples. The sign

could not be missed; only women carried water jars. *The prediction of the betrayal (14:17-21)* shows Jesus' full knowledge of the events and by implication his control of events. The allusion to the treachery of a table companion is based on Psalm 41:10. *The institution of the Eucharist (14:22-25)* is a liturgical formula, identified by scholars with a Jerusalem or Palestinian liturgy; Matthew 26:26-29 is close to Mark. The Eucharist is an anticipation and a sign of the messianic banquet.

The theme of Jesus' knowledge of events is repeated in *the prediction of the flight of the disciples and the denial of Peter (14:26-31)*. There is no allusion to different night watches or different times at which the cock crows; Peter's fall will occur so suddenly that the cock will not have time to repeat his crowing. *The Gethsemane narrative (14:32-42)* realistically portrays the human feelings of Jesus and his final acceptance of the will of his father; it is a mistake to take this as anything but a genuine emotional struggle. But since the witnesses were dozing, the narrative must contain some degree of reconstruction. The three are the same three who witnessed the transfiguration (9:2). *The arrest of Jesus (14:43-52)* was affected by a "crowd" (43); Mark has no reference to priests, temple police or Roman soldiers (Luke 22:52; John 18:2). The words of Jesus check the threat of violence; he is master of the events. The young man who saw the incident is mentioned only by Mark, and he has traditionally been identified with Mark; but the text offers no base for this conjecture.

The Trial of Jesus

The trial of Jesus before the Sanhedrin (14:53-65) involves difficulties both with history and with the variations in the different Gospels; and a number of modern scholars believe that Mark's two sessions are a doublet of a single session held in the morning. Here Jesus finally reveals the messianic secret when asked by the supreme religious authorities of Judaism. Neither a claim of messiahship nor a prediction of the destruction of the temple would be blasphemy; the use of the Son of Man text of Daniel 7:13 could be so regarded. But Jesus had taught that the Messiah must suffer; and the use of the text promises vindication after suffering. In its present form, however, the text expresses the developed messianic faith of the early apostolic church. Mark identifies those who mocked Jesus as the members of the Sanhedrin. *The denials of Peter (14:66-72)* are narrated with variations in the four Gospels. Mark's account is obviously climactic, going from a profession of ignorance to denial with imprecations.

The hearing before Pilate (15:1-15) dealt with the charge that Jesus claimed kingship; this was a legitimate translation of Messiah for a Roman. (See above for the suggestion that the morning session of the Sanhedrin was the only session.) Crucifixion, inflicted on slaves and non-Romans, was the penalty for murder, robbery, rebellion and treason. The practice of amnesty mentioned here is not supported by other sources; but such practices were not unknown in Roman administration. Barabbas, as a bandit rebel, was a type of popular hero often found in the Near East in modern, as well as in ancient, times. Mark represents Pilate as yielding to popular pressure. This is not in harmony with the character of Pilate as Josephus represents him, but Josephus does not deserve implicit faith. *The mocking of Jesus (15:16-20)* was an echo of the charge of the claim to royalty. The "purple" garment was probably the red cloak of a Roman soldier, and the crown of thorns was a radiate crown (like that represented on the Statue of Liberty), not the wreath so common in Christian art.

The pressed service of Simon of Cyrene in *the way of the cross (15:21-22)* suggests the weariness of Jesus. It was not the cross which was carried, but the transverse beam; the upright beam stood permanently at the place of execution. Alexander and Rufus are thought to be members of the Roman Christian community, for whom Mark wrote. Before *the crucifixion (15:23-27)* Jesus was offered a nar-

cotic drink which he refused. Mark's "third hour" is somewhat ambiguous; the legal process could hardly have been
finished by 9:00 A.M., and hence it should mean the late
morning. The charge on which the criminal was condemned was worn by him or affixed to the cross. *The
mocking of Jesus (15:29-32),* in which the most distinguished Jewish leaders took part, echoes the saying about
the temple and the claim of messiahship.

The death of Jesus (15:33-39) is preceded by a quotation
of Psalm 22:1. It is uncertain whether this is a deliberate
choice of a psalm in which the afflicted petitioner is
finally vindicated or whether it reveals a profound spiritual
desolation of Jesus which is beyond commentary. Jesus
was offered a sip of cheap wine (not "vinegar"). It has been
noticed that men in exhaustion do not die with a loud cry;
and it is suggested that this was a response to some sudden
and acute pain. The rending of the veil may be a symbolic
allusion to the redeeming death as the event which opens
a single way of salvation to all men. This may be the basis
of the allusions to the veil in Hebrews 6:19-20 and 10:
19-20 (for a similar thought compare Ephesians 2:14). At
this moment of the accomplishment of the mission of the
Messiah a Gentile confesses that Jesus was the son of God.
The presence of the women (15:40-41) looks forward to
the narrative of the empty tomb. Death by crucifixion was
normally lingering, perhaps protracted over a few days,
and the death of Jesus was unexpected. In *the burial narrative (15:42-47)* the contrast between the unknown Joseph
of Arimathea and the Eleven who had fled is obvious; but
more important is the affirmation that Jesus really died
and was really buried in a tomb behind a large stone which
effectively barricaded the entrance.

The resurrection account (16:1-8) breaks off so abruptly
that many scholars believe part of it has been lost. There
is a reference to a meeting in Galilee which Mark does not
mention, and there is no apparition to any one. The most
important MSS. end at 16:8. Yet Mark exhibits a faith in

the resurrection which is no less than the faith found in
any other Gospel. What is left is the basic affirmation of
the empty tomb. This does not of itself prove that Jesus
rose, but it makes faith in the resurrection possible; at the
same time it obliges one who denies the resurrection to
find the body. *The present conclusion of Mark (16:9-20)*
cannot be the work of Mark himself. It is merely a summary of incidents which are related in the other three
Gospels with independent additions. It does not, as we
have noticed, include the apparition in Galilee. It was very
probably composed as a replacement for the lost portion
of Mark; the abruptness and brevity of Mark, compared
with the other three Gospels, suggested that this expansion should be constructed from the others.

Eschatology

A modern interpreter wrote a few years ago that "eschatology" is an uncouth word, and most Christians would
agree with him; they find the word difficult to spell and
impossible to define. Yet children used to be taught the
four last things as the only sure things. Nowadays many of
us are less sure. Still one must wonder how it is all going
to come out; and the answer to that wonder is eschatology,
which in its simplest form is an affirmation that it will
come out, that history will end. A little reflection will show
that if it does not, God is either not real or he is inactive.

The Gospel of Mark has the earliest form of Christian
eschatology. Our commentary has attempted to indicate
what could be shown in great detail, that much of the
earliest "Christian" eschatology was actually Jewish. The
major image in Mark's picture, the coming of the Son of
Man in the clouds of heaven, is lifted straight out of the
book of Daniel; and hardly any interpreter doubts that the
Son of Man in Daniel is the Jewish people. We notice in
reading Matthew that Jesus is often the new Israel, so
there is nothing extraordinary in the use of this text. More
significant is the fact that this is really all of Mark's escha-

tology: Jesus will return as saviour and lord in a form which no one can fail to recognize.

Now some questions. Assuming that the image drawn from Daniel is just that, an image, can we conjecture the form of the historical reality which the image signifies? Caution recommends that we do not try. The passage expresses the earliest Christian faith that the work of God is frustrated if Jesus is not ultimately recognized as saviour and lord by all men. The only historical process mentioned in connection with revelation is the proclamation of the gospel to all men. Perhaps we should reflect on this saying, not only on "all men," but also on "this gospel." Has the church proclaimed the whole gospel to all men? Not yet, really, neither whole nor to all. When it does, there will certainly be a new and unparalleled revelation of the reality of Jesus for which the image of a coming on clouds will seem less exaggerated than it seems now. But it will not be a new saving act; it will be the recognition that the death and resurrection of Jesus are, in the words of Rudolf Bultmann, "the decisive eschatological act of God in Christ."

Difficulties

The reader of the Gospels who stops to reflect is going to be disturbed that the earliest account of the passion, death and resurrection of Jesus is as full of holes as it is. It seemed only honest to point out these features in the commentary. Much, of course, depends on what Mark says clearly, that none of the disciples were present at the process. The devout reader has long leaned on the belief that the risen Jesus told the disciples in full detail just what happened. The Gospels were not written by men who had heard the full details from anyone. If Jesus ever gave the disciples the authentic version, they proceeded to forget it.

One by-product of this is that it is never possible to argue with Jewish scholars who say that Jews had no part in the death of Jesus. One can point out that this claim ultimately imposes the conclusion that we know nothing of the death of Jesus, and that the type of historical argument employed could be used to show that Jesus died of old age. But the passion narrative remains a hearsay account, although I do not believe the disciples were entirely uninformed about the events.

The significance of the death was more important in the early proclamation than in the details. If the death of Jesus was the saving act of God in Christ by which all men are delivered from their sins, then all men stand with the executioners, where Christian preachers have long set them. This was clear to Paul, who wrote before Mark, and he tried to make it clear to those Jews and Gentiles to whom he preached and wrote his letters.

We have pointed out that Mark's account of the resurrection is so unsatisfactory that many scholars believe that part of it has been lost. Again we sense an unkind fortune which keeps from us the earliest written account of the climactic saving event, the event of which Paul said that if Jesus has not risen, our faith is vain and we are still dead in our sins. But our faith would be no greater nor more meaningful if we had a first person account from Peter, fully authenticated and notarized. There is no history of the resurrection as the climactic saving event by which all men rise to a new life.

Chapter Twelve

INTRODUCTION TO LUKE

The Authorship of Luke

The third of the Synoptic Gospels is by general agreement the latest; it does not betray its date, but scholars put it between 80 and 90 A.D. Some of their reasons for this opinion are drawn from the dangerous critical view that Luke shows a more developed understanding of the gospel than Matthew and Mark. The view is dangerous because it pre-supposes a complete understanding of the process of development, and we do not know the apostolic church that well. Nevertheless, the impression that Luke is later than the other two comes in strongly, and there are serious difficulties in attempting to place the Gospel earlier.

If the author is correctly identified with the Luke mentioned in the New Testament, he must have been an old man when the Gospel was written. This too involves certain difficulties, which have moved some modern scholars to suppose that our "Luke" is a second revised and enlarged edition of a "Proto-Luke." This theory, in the opinion of most scholars, raises more questions than it answers; but it shows that one cannot simply date Luke at the period mentioned without implying some difficulties.

The Luke of the New Testament was a companion of Paul (Colossians 4:14; Philemon 24; 2 Timothy 4:11). Of these texts only Philemon is surely from Paul, but the association of Luke and Paul is established. There is no good reason to doubt that he was a physician, although efforts to find the Hellenistic medical vocabulary in his writings have not succeeded. It has been noticed that Luke

(8:43) softens Mark's severe criticism of the medical profession (5:26); but Matthew leaves out the offensive sentence entirely. As we shall see, Luke is also the author of Acts; and this book discloses that he accompanied Paul on one of his journeys. It should also be noted that Luke seems to have thought of the Gospel and Acts as a single work, and consequently there are certain matching features. The other Gospels are not so conceived and written, and we have suggested that Mark thought that the "Gospel" ended with the empty tomb.

It is not easy to conjecture the place of composition of Luke; it is clear that Luke was a Gentile and that he wrote for Gentiles. Luke did not know much about Judaism nor much about Palestinian geography and Palestinian life. His conversion of the beaten-earth roof of a Palestinian house into a tiled roof is celebrated (Mark 2:4; Luke 5:19); apparently he had not only never seen an earth roof but could not even grasp the idea, and he serenely wrote that the bearers let the sick man down "through the tiles." There is a widely accepted conjecture that Luke came from Antioch. It appears that this great city of Syria had the first largely Gentile community; the foundation of the church of Antioch is related in Acts 11:19-26, and this church sent Paul and Barnabas on their first mission (Acts 13:1-3). But neither in the Gospel nor in Acts does Luke betray his origin; and if he came from Antioch, he could have had almost any ethnic affiliation.

Thus the interest of the Gospel together with Acts is to show how the good news reached the Gentile world. This interest will appear in several of the details which we indicate below. Luke's lack of interest in Judaism and lack of knowledge, however, may reflect something deeper than mere Gentile self-interest. Luke was in possession of information about the controversies between Jewish Christians and Gentile Christians; these controversies appeared both in his sources (Mark and the sayings of Jesus) and in his own material, including the book of Acts. If the date of

the Gospel is as late as 80-90, very probably the Jewish
controversy had lost most of its vigor and interest. Luke
may have thought of himself not only as a speaker to the
Gentiles, but also as an agent of reconciliation between
Jewish and Gentile Christians. The controversial sharpness
of Matthew and Mark is notably softened in Luke. His
solution of the mystery of Jewish unbelief is the same as
Paul's solution; Jewish unbelief became the occasion of
the proclamation of the Gospel to the Gentiles.

The question of the sources of Luke is of some peculiar
interest because Luke has so much material of his own.
The Gospel has 1149 verses. Luke uses 350 of the 661
verses of Matthew. He has 325 verses in common with
Matthew—the material known as Q. Thus the remaining
474 verses are peculiar to Luke. Much of this belongs to
the infancy and the resurrection narratives. There is another large block of matter called the "journey narrative"
(9:51—19:27). Luke has accepted Mark's arrangement of
Galilee—journey—Jerusalem. In Mark the journey is
covered in 10:1-52. Luke, is seems, was embarrassed by a
wealth of material for which there was no place in Mark's
scheme. He inserted it in the only place where there was
room for expansion, and thus the journey narrative has
become almost as long as that part of the Gospel which
precedes it. If Luke wrote at the date most commonly proposed for the Gospel, the peculiar material very improb-
ably came from personal investigation of living memories;
not many could have survived to that time. If he used documents, their origin then becomes a problem which has
not been solved.

A Gospel for Gentiles

Luke's use of Mark has some peculiarities also. He
omits Mark 6:45—8:26, and the question arises whether he
had it. Modern scholars do not doubt that he did have it;
for they see in other omissions of the material of Mark a
principle which, when considered, is revealing about

Luke's vision of his own role. Luke did not use sayings or episodes which were similar in content, theme or expression to sayings or episodes which he had already used. Thus Luke seems to have thought of himself as an expositor rather than as a historian. Other omissions can often be explained from his unwillingness to use material which was unintelligible or offensive to Gentiles; among the Gentiles who did not understand or were offended there was, of course, Luke himself. Manifestations of this Gentile sensibility are the omissions of the discussion of clean and unclean (Mark 7:1-23), the harsh exchange between Jesus and the Gentile woman (Mark 7:24-30, really a good example of Palestinian wisdom as an exchange of wit), the cure of the deaf-mute (Mark 7:31-37, offensive because of the use of spittle), and the cure of the blind man of Bethsaida (Mark 8:22-26, difficult because the cure was gradual and because spittle was used). If these explanations are correct, then Luke allowed himself a freedom of selection which is barely tolerable to an expositor and unpardonable in a historian. Plainly he was under no compulsion to tell everything he knew.

Luke alone of the evangelists has a description of his role (1:1-4). This preface can be recognized as written in the conventional style of Greek and Hellenistic historians; and the use of the style does not prove that Luke thought of himself as a Greek or Hellenistic historian. It does show, however, that Luke was not unacquainted with historical writing. In fact he wrote that singular and unparalleled type of narrative called a gospel. It is impossible to determine who is meant by the "many" who had written before him. He knew Mark but almost certainly did not know Matthew. It is uncertain, as we have noticed, how wide and how close his knowledge of the "eyewitnesses" was. The "closeness" or "accuracy" of his investigations can be tested only by his use of Mark, about which certain reservations must be made. His "orderly account" was a following of Mark's order except for his own material.

These reflections seem to make it clear that Luke used conventional purpose without sharing the intentions of those who invented the language. His purpose, he says in the concluding line, is to show Theophilus the "security" of the things in which he has been instructed. "Security" here must mean credibility; Theophilus has been instructed in events, and Luke wishes to give him a full account of the events, somewhat tailored to suit his Gentile sensibilities, even to the point of omitting what he deemed better left unmentioned. Nor should we patronize the Gentile sensibilities, if it was through respect for these that Luke omitted such crudities as the execution of John the Baptist (Mark 6:17-29) and the scourging of Jesus (Mark 15:15). Luke has a certain delicacy of his own, shown in the omission of the full harsh quotations of Isaiah 6:9-10 (Mark 4:12), the hyperboles of renunciation (Mark 9:43-48, the hand, the eye and the foot), the curse of the traitor (Mark 14:21), the kiss of Judas (Mark 14:45), and some details of the abusive treatment of Jesus (Mark 14:65).

A Gospel Chronology

On the other hand, Luke is the only evangelist who gives any dates, and in this he is more of the historian than the others. It is true that one of his dates cannot be correct; the census of Quirinius cannot have occurred in the year of the birth of Jesus (2:2), and Luke was either misinformed or he misunderstood his sources. He gives the age of Jesus at the beginning of his public life as about thirty (3:23), and it has been impossible to make it more precise. His synchronism is not as clear to us as it was to him—or at least not as clear to him as he thought it was (3:1-2). We can check only the fifteenth year of Tiberius Caesar; and since there were variant calculations which may have influenced Luke, this could be either 27-28 or 28-29, we should still have to ask the source of a date so precise.

The connection of the Gospel with Acts as two parts of a single work has given the ascension of Jesus a theological significance which it does not have elsewhere in the New Testament; for no other New Testament writer distinguishes the ascension as an event. In the other Gospels and in the Epistles the ascension cannot be distinguished from the resurrection and the glorification of Jesus; and for both of these there are no witnesses except in the writings of Luke. For Luke the ascension of Jesus means the coming of the Spirit; and Jesus lives in the church because the Spirit dwells in the church. This is very close to the theology of the Spirit in Paul, and it is not difficult to establish associations between the two here. But Paul does not have the ascension of Jesus as the point where Jesus ceases to exist on earth and begins to exist in the church. There is also an association with the theology of the Spirit in John (John 14:26; 15:26; 16:13-14): the coming of the Spirit is conditioned on the return of Jesus to the Father, which in John is not an ascension. Luke's awareness of the Spirit appears in a few other changes he makes in his sources. Where the Father gives good things in Matthew (7:11), in Luke he gives the Spirit (5:13). The Spirit overshadows Mary at the conception of Jesus (1:35). Jesus, full of the Spirit, was led by the Spirit into the desert (4:1); here Luke softens Mark's harsh saying that the Spirit drove Jesus into the desert (1:12). Jesus entered Capernaum in the Spirit (4:14). Only Luke (4:18) in the narrative of Jesus at Nazareth presents Jesus as reading Isaiah 61:1, "The Spirit of the Lord is upon me." Luke adds that Jesus rejoiced in the Spirit (10:21 in contrast with Matthew 11:25). The theme of the Spirit will recur in Acts; Luke anticipates it in the Gospel.

It is a corollary of Luke's interest in the church in the Gentile world that eschatology becomes more remote in his Gospel than it is in Mark or Matthew. In Luke's version of "the Synoptic Apocalypse" there is a clear distinction between the fall of Jerusalem (21:20-24) and the Parousia

(21:25-28) which is not found in Matthew and Mark; Luke was more obviously written after the fall of Jerusalem than Matthew and Mark. Luke recognizes that the fulfillment of the apostolic mission to the Gentiles does not permit the expectation of an imminent Parousia. Quite possibly this is connected with the appearance of the ascension in Luke; in the other Gospels the glorification of Jesus is not distinguished from the Parousia. So also the Reign of God is not purely eschatological; this is not peculiar to Luke, for it is not purely eschatological in Mark or Matthew either, but Luke has a few sayings of his own. Such is 17:20-21, which can be paraphrased: The Reign of God does not come in a way which can be observed, nor can one point and say it is here or there; it is right here in your midst. Most probably the saying is a cryptic identification of Jesus himself with the Reign, an identification made elsewhere in the New Testament as well. But the non-eschatological character of the Reign is emphasized; it does not appear "in a cloud with power and great glory" (21:27). The Reign of God begins with the appearance of Jesus in the flesh and not with the Second Coming.

It is also connected with the theme of the church that the transformation of the disciples from Mark goes even beyond the transformation which they experience in Matthew. Luke, as we have seen, was ready to take liberties with Mark when the material was difficult or offensive. Plainly the dullness and incredulity of the disciples were both difficult and offensive. Only Luke adds to a saying found in Matthew (19:28) that Jesus appoints for the disciples, who have persevered with him through his temptations, a kingdom, as the father has appointed a kingdom for Jesus (22:28-29). One cannot suspect that Luke is being ironical in locating this saying in the last supper just before the disciples abandoned Jesus. In fact the explicit statement that the disciples abandoned him and fled (Mark 14:52; Matthew 26:56) is omitted by Luke, surely a rather futile effort to spare the disciples some embarrassment. In

Luke the disciples, far from presenting obstacles by their slowness of wit and their slowness to believe, become real "disciples"—that is, Jesus trains them for their role. Peter's rebuke of Jesus for announcing his passion is omitted by Luke (Mark 9:32-33; Matthew 16:22-23). The question of the disciples after the healing of the epileptic child (Mark 9:28-29) is omitted (Luke 9:43); even Matthew (17:20) explains the failure of the disciples as due to their lack of faith. The misunderstanding of the saying about leaven (Mark 8:14-21; Matthew 16:5-12) is completely omitted by Luke (12:1). The failure to understand the prediction of the passion (Mark 9:32) is softened by the addition that "the word was hidden from them" (9:45). The embarrassing request of the sons of Zebedee (Mark 10:35-40) is also omitted, although Luke retains some of the sayings addressed to the disciples about ambition and the lust for power.

Yet Luke does not remove entirely the theme of the failure of the disciples. Even if he thought of himself as an expositor rather than a historian, it was not his purpose to falsify history. Both Luke and Matthew could allege that Mark's portrayal of the disciples did not portray their place in the church in its fullness. What they became after the resurrection was pertinent, and the narrative should not be left as if nothing had happened to transform them. Luke alone has the story about the two swords (22:35-38). In no hypothesis could Luke have meant to imply that the sword would have anything to do with the establishment of the reign. The conversation can be nothing but an instance of a gross misunderstanding of the disciples concerning the kingdom. This misunderstanding Luke did not attempt to conceal. In the narrative of the two disciples traveling to Emmaus, one of them says that he had hoped that it was Jesus who would deliver Israel (24:21). The theme is expressed again in Acts 1:6. The importance of the disciples in these passages was that they had passed from unbelief to lasting belief. This they could teach the members of the church both by word and by example.

A Gospel with Feeling

Perhaps interpreters of the Gospel are being insensitive
to Mark when they say that he is unstudied; he does appear less studied than Matthew. But when we encounter
Luke we surely encounter conscious art. The historian—
in contrast to the novelist—is not entitled to mention the
inner feelings of his characters, but only the manifestation
of feelings. Luke the conscious historian often uses the
privilege of the novelist. He notes that people heard Jesus
with expectation (3:15). People "glorified" him (4:15), a
remark perhaps substantially accurate but certainly un-
verified. He notes that the witnesses of a cure were as-
tonished (9:43). Matthew gives the Lord's prayer in the
sermon on the mount; Luke presents it as the answer to a
request elicited by the sight of Jesus at prayer (11:1). The
saying about the evil generation is given when Jesus sees
that the crowds around him are growing (11:29). The saying about repentance is set in a context of conversation
concerning sudden mass disasters, and the context certainly gives the saying a psychological impact (13:1-5). The
saying about the kingdom of God "in your midst" is uttered
in a roughly similar manner as a response to quite a different question (17:20-21). Two parables are introduced
with a statement of the sentiments against which the parables are directed (18:1,9). Another parable is addressed to
the unspoken sentiments of the disciples (19:1). Such features in Luke's composition are partly due to a desire for
vividness and an effort to create in words the psychological
context and the impact of the words of Jesus. In a few of
the instances there is also a conscious effort to recreate
the surprise, even the shock when the words of Jesus go
beyond what is expected. We see here an imaginative reconstruction of the material which Luke found in his
sources. In addition, we can see in Luke a sensitivity to
persons and their feelings, a sensitivity which is not evident in Mark or in Matthew.

Luke has the most explicitly universalistic outlook of all

the Gospels; this is not surprising since Luke is the only evangelist whom we are sure was a Gentile. Luke's universalism is not confined to Gentiles, although this element is clearly present in passages not paralleled in Matthew and Mark. Jesus is announced as a light to the Gentiles (2:32, a phrase based on Isaiah 42:6 and 49:6). Luke quotes Isaiah 40:5 "All flesh shall see God's salvation" (3:6). In a parable (10:29-37) and a healing story (17:11-19) Samaritans appear in a favorable light. It seems that Luke must have received these items from his sources, for it is improbable that Luke, so poorly informed in many areas of Palestinian Judaism, should have been personally acquainted with the feud between Jews and Samaritans. It is also improbable that these two passages should have been as meaningful to Gentiles as they were to Jews. Matthew mentions Samaritans once, Mark mentions neither Samaria nor Samaritans; John, however, uses this element of universalism (4:1-42). The universalism of Luke is social as well as ethnic, and consequently this deserves closer attention.

The Mercy Parables

Luke, more than the other evangelists, brings out the associations of Jesus with sinners and outcasts. Once Luke says the Pharisees grumbled because Jesus received sinners and ate with them (15:1-2, similar to the dinner given by Levi/Matthew in Matthew 9:9-13 and Mark 2:13-17). This theme is elaborated in the "mercy parables" and what may be called the mercy episodes of Luke. Most of the mercy parables are found in Luke 15; these include such well-known parables as the lost sheep, the lost coin and the prodigal son. Luke explains in so many words that there is greater joy in heaven for one repentant sinner than for ninety-nine righteous who need no repentance; and it seems that in Luke's revision of this sentence an implicit criticism is leveled at the self-righteous who do not recognize their own guilt. Also, the same criticism is the theme of the parable of the Pharisee and the tax-collector (18:9-14).

Kindness to sinners and outcasts is also brought out in Luke's narratives. All three evangelists have the incident of the woman who anointed the hair of Jesus (Matthew 26:6-13; Mark 14:3-9; Luke 7:36-50). Only Luke says that she washed his feet with her tears—a hyperbole, surely —and that she was a sinner in the city. The variations are sufficient to make interpreters wonder whether Luke is using Mark or another source; but Luke's version certainly contrasts the forgiveness of Jesus with the righteousness of his host. Luke also relates that Jesus invited himself to dinner in the home of Zacchaeus (19:1-10). Matthew's saying that the disciples should be perfect as the Father is perfect (Matthew 5:48) becomes a saying that they should be merciful as the Father is merciful (6:36).

In pointing out these Lucan emphases we do not imply that the themes of mercy and forgiveness and of openness to the undesirable of society are not found in the other synoptic Gospels. But one cannot help noticing that the passages cited have no parallels in Matthew and Mark, and one may ask why the emphasis is greater in Luke. It is a hazardous guess that the Jewish Christian community retained some of the elements of Pharisaism which elicited such passages as Matthew 23; and indeed one need not appeal to Pharisaism to explain self-righteousness and unwillingness to forgive in the Christian community at any period of its history. We have noticed that at the date when Luke was most probably written the Jewish community had ceased to be very important in the church. It is not impossible that the Jewish opinion which identified Gentile with sinner had not ceased within the apostolic church. The emphasis which Luke gives this theme is not directed at a vacuum.

The poor are the objects of compassion in all the Gospels; again Luke has passages of his own. He alone quotes Isaiah 61:1 in the incident of the Nazareth synagogue

(4:18), in which the speaker announces that he proclaims good news to the poor. "The poor in spirit" of Matthew 5:3 have often been misinterpreted as those who are spiritually detached from their wealth; Luke removes all ambiguity by restating the beatitude of the poor (6:20) and adding a woe to the rich (6:24). Only Luke has the parable of Dives and Lazarus (16:19-31); and nowhere in the Gospels is there any more severe condemnation than in this parable, in which the guilty man actually does nothing. And it is precisely because he has done nothing that he is so severely condemned. In the parable of the rich man who builds bigger barns to store his wealth, the rich man is dismissed with the appellation of fool (12:13-21).

It is scarcely unrelated to Luke's treatment of poverty that his sayings about renunciation are more rigorously couched than they are in Matthew and Mark. While the disciples abandon the boat and their father in Matthew (4:22) and Mark (1:20), in Luke they abandon all things (5:11). This is not as peculiar as it may seem, for in all three Gospels Peter says later that they have left all things (Matthew 19:27; Mark 10:28; Luke 18:28 has "our own"). But peculiar to Luke is the saying that one may not put his hand to the plow and look back (9:62). Where Matthew speaks of those who love their families more than Jesus (10:37), Luke uses a Semitic rather than a Greek idiom and demands that the disciples hate their families (14:26). The saying, "Sell what you have and give alms" (12:33), has no parallel except in the story of the rich young man (Matthew 19:21; Mark 10:21; Luke 18:22), where its application is less obviously general. All three evangelists have the saying that the disciple must take up his cross (Matthew 16:24; Mark 8:34; Luke 9:23); only Luke adds that the disciple must do this "each day." The themes of poverty and renunciation are also expressed in Acts. Luke describes the Jerusalem church as practicing renunciation and community of goods (Acts 4:32-37), and obviously regards this as the model Christian community. No other New Testament writer mentions the practice either at Jerusalem or in any other community, and it is very probable that Luke has idealized the Jerusalem church in this respect.

We have emphases on poverty and renunciation, as we have on sin and forgiveness, which are not paralleled in the other Gospels; and we have to ask about these emphases also. It is evident from many allusions both in the New Testament and in early Christian literature that the membership of the apostolic and the post-apostolic church was drawn from the lower classes, even from slaves. Christianity was what, in modern times, would be called a proletarian movement, even an underground movement. Thus it is rarely reflected in literature and history during its first two centuries; the educated and the ruling classes took very little interest in the religious activities of the lower classes, especially when these activities were oriental and erotic. The educated and the ruling classes in the Roman world were largely irreligious.

The Gospel of Luke may betray a certain self-consciousness in the Christians of the apostolic church that they belonged to the masses, those who had no influence on the great world. Certainly Paul spoke brutally about the social qualities of his Christians; there were among them not many wise, not many powerful, not many noble (1 Corinthians 1:26). In the Gentile world of Luke the difference between the wealthy and the ruling classes on the one hand and the poor and slaves on the other was deeper than it was in Judaism, which always retained a kind of social democracy. To Luke it was even more remarkable that God should have revealed himself to the poor and the foolish of the world; and the implication is clear that the rich cannot accept the revelation of God unless they divest themselves of their wealth. We can be assured that this message comes not from Luke but from Jesus, for it is as novel and as contrary to conventions as anything in the

New Testament; and it is, of course, found in all three Gospels. Luke shows us that this part of the Gospel proclamation fell on good soil in the proletarian and slave populations of the great cities of the Roman Empire.

Jesus and Prayer

Luke mentions prayer more frequently than the other evangelists. Jesus prayed at his baptism (3:21). He prayed all night before the choice of the Twelve (6:12), a critical moment, but prayer is not mentioned by Mark or Matthew. He prayed before the confession of Peter (9:18), another critical moment; and here Luke explicitly says that Jesus prayed alone. Jesus took the three disciples up to the mountain for prayer before the transfiguration (9:28). The formula of the Lord's prayer was given in answer to a request that Jesus teach the disciples to pray, a request elicited by the sight of Jesus at prayer (11:1). Only Luke has the parable of the wicked judge, an encouragement to perseverance in prayer (18:1-8). There is a textual problem in Luke 22:43-44, which describes the prolongation of the agony of Jesus and the bloody sweat; these verses are not found in the most important manuscripts, and there is no consensus among textual critics. Several argue that the verses are more likely to be omitted than added, an observation which has probability but which lacks conviction. Thus the most human picture that we have of Jesus at prayer is unfortunately without sure support in the textual evidence.

Luke's interest in prayer very probably reflects a more developed community cult than the earlier Gospels reflect. We know of no Christian assembly from the beginning which was not an assembly for worship, but some time must have elapsed before the worship acquired a ritual character. Prayer would not have been peculiarly Christian, of course; Jewish worship both in the synagogue and in the temple was conducted according to traditional ritual, and long prayers were employed. Matthew's saying on prayer (6:5-8) has no parallel in either Mark or Luke, and indeed may seem to be in some opposition with Luke. The saying of Matthew is quite explicit in rejecting public prayer and in discouraging lengthy prayer. Luke does not encourage either of these; and from the beginning, Christian tradition has not understood the saying of Matthew as a prohibition of cultic worship but rather of ostentatious personal prayer. Luke exhibits what has become a traditional Christian piety, the belief that at critical and solemn moments, moments of personal suffering and personal decision, the believer invokes God personally in the assurance that God hears personal prayer.

We have alluded, in discussing the other Gospels, to certain transformations in the character of Jesus in the direction of blurring his humanity and emphasizing his superhuman features. This is continued in Luke, and it demands no special comment; but it should be added that the Gospel furnished some explanation, if not genuine historical foundation, for the tradition that Luke was a painter. While he does not have the vividness in detail of Mark, he has furnished more scenes for Christian artists than any other Gospel; and one can say only that Luke's scenes can often be visualized. One recalls such favorite scenes as the infancy stories, the widow of Nain, the woman in the house of Simon, the good Samaritan, Mary and Martha, the prodigal son, Dives and Lazarus, Zacchaeus, the penitent thief and the disciples at Emmaus, and one realizes how much art Luke has inspired. It is not vividness in detail that makes Luke's pictures. One suspects that it is rather the tone of serenity which prevails in so much of the Gospel.

The conflicts of Jesus with the Pharisees have grown dim with the passage of time. Luke is aware of the passion, but he lives in the church of the risen Lord and the Spirit. Jesus is the prophet and the savior who dispenses joy and comfort by his presence, by his teaching and by his healing. If there is one title more than another which distinguishes Jesus as he appears in Luke, it is Savior: savior from disease, savior from sin, savior from the sorrow of the world. The Gospel of Luke is the Gospel of hope.

Chapter Thirteen

THE GOSPEL OF LUKE, CHAPTERS 1–6

Luke's Sources

The prologue (1:1-4) is written in the style of Hellenistic Greek literature, especially Hellenistic history. The style shows that Luke was acquainted with these literary works; but this style is abandoned after the prologue and does not reappear until the prologue of Acts. This as much as anything else shows Luke's dependence on his sources; it may also suggest that by the time Luke wrote, a certain "gospel style" had arisen. The mysterious Theophilus is unknown; the title "excellent" suggests a person of some rank. Luke himself was not an "eyewitness" but depended upon the apostolic witness.

Matthew and Luke both have infancy gospels. It is evident from a simple reading that they do not depend on a single source. The problems involved are best handled, in the present state of knowledge, by treating both Gospels as independent reconstructions with no close dependence on authentic memory, written with a theological rather than a historical purpose. There is in Luke a certain obvious balance between the accounts of the birth of John the Baptist and the birth of Jesus. *The birth of John the Baptist is announced (1:5-25);* for the details one may compare the announcement of the birth of Samson (Judges 13:1-25) and the Old Testament references to sterile women who received children as a promise from God: Sarah, Rebekah, Rachel and Hannah. The request of Zechariah for a sign is punished in a rather surprising way; see Abraham (Genesis

15:3-8), Gideon (Judges 6:11-24+36-40). The angel Gabriel
is derived from Daniel 8:16-26+9:21-27; in Daniel, Gabriel
is the herald of the saving act of God.

The birth of Jesus is also announced (1:26-38); but it is
announced to the mother, not to the father. In Matthew's
infancy narrative Joseph is the chief actor; in Luke Mary
speaks and acts. It is in the annunciation narrative rather
than in the birth narrative that Luke affirms the virgin
conception. Mary's question elicits the affirmation; her
question is not, like the question of Zechariah, a request
for a sign. The promised son is identified as the messianic
king; the faith of the Christian community gave the title
"son of the Most High" a fullness it did not have in 2
Samuel 2:7 and Psalms 2:7 and 89:27.

The story of the visitation (1:39-55) not only connects
the births of Jesus and John but makes John the witness of
Jesus while he is still in the womb. The hymn of Mary (the
Magnificat) is largely composed from Old Testament texts
(see the margin of the *Jerusalem Bible*). It is thought to be
an early Christian hymn; strangely it contains no messianic allusion. *The birth of John the Baptist (1:57-66)*
releases Zechariah from his dumbness. The name of John
seems to have a significance which eludes the commentators, as it possibly eluded Luke; in the narrative the
conferring of the name is simply a fulfillment of the sign
declared in the words of the angel Gabriel. *The hymn of
Zechariah (1:67-79)*, the *Benedictus*, is thought to be a
Jewish-Christian hymn or a Jewish hymn with a Christian
addition; unlike the *Magnificat* of Mary (see above), it does
include clear messianic allusions.

Historical Problems

The birth of Jesus (2:1-20) as narrated by Luke contains
a number of unsolved historical problems. We know of no
general Roman census which occurred at an acceptable
date and included Palestine; the memory of Luke's sources
had failed here. The tradition of the birth of Jesus in

Bethlehem was not easily reconciled with his known residence at Nazareth, and Luke's sources offered an early explanation of this difficulty. A display of messianic glory is related which has no echo anywhere in the Gospels. The narrative is best taken as theological symbolism expressing one of Luke's favorite themes; the Messiah is himself born as one of the poor, and he is recognized not by the great and the wise but by the poor. The theme recurs in the following episodes of *Simeon and Anna (2:22-38);* Simeon also recognizes the Messiah as the Suffering Servant. These two witnesses are typical figures of the devout Jewish man and woman who lived in fidelity to their obligations and in the hope that God would deliver his people as he had promised. They are certainly intended to stand in contrast with the Pharisees and the Sadducees, who rejected the fulfillment of the hope which Jesus revealed. The statement of *the growth of Jesus (2:39-40+2:51-52)* is a doublet; the two sentences are separated by the story of *Jesus in the temple (2:41-50).* Jewish boys were expected to undertake the full observance of the Law at the age of puberty, 12-13 years—the beginning of adulthood symbolized ritually by the modern *bar mitzvah* ceremony. Jesus appears as a good Jew who has an adult understanding of the Law at the earliest possible age.

The ministry of John the Baptist (3:1-18) is dated by Luke with a fullness of detail not all of which is useful to the historian for lack of sufficient data. The date can be either 26 or 28 A.D. Luke parallels Mark and Matthew except in 3:10-15, which is peculiar to himself; this is addressed to the poor, among whom are included soldiers, usually the means of oppression for the wealthy. Luke places here the story of *the arrest of John (3:19-20),* which Matthew and Mark combine with the account of John's execution; all agree that Jesus did not begin his own ministry before the arrest of John. Luke omits the story of Herod's feast and John's execution; commentators believe that he found it too crude and barbarous to repeat. In the

story of *the baptism of Jesus (3:21-22)* Luke, implies that
the spirit was visible to others besides Jesus; and Luke
alone uses the words of the heavenly voice from Psalm
2:7.

The genealogy of Jesus (3:23-38) for the period from
David to Jesus differs entirely from Matthew's genealogy;
before David, both depend on the Old Testament. There is
no convincing explanation of the difference, and both
genealogies are highly artificial. Luke goes back to Adam,
again depending on the Old Testament, while Matthew
begins with Abraham; this is thought to show a wider
human view of the scope of the saving act of God in
Jesus.

The temptations of Jesus (4:1-13), which Luke has in
common with Matthew, are messianic temptations; they
come to the church, but they have already been overcome
by Jesus, and overcome in each instance by a quotation
from the Old Testament. The order of Matthew seems
more climactic to the modern reader, but it suits the theology of Matthew as well as Luke's order suits the theology
of Luke; and one should not too quickly assume that Luke
"changed" the original order. In Luke's Gospel, Jerusalem
has a central position; the Gospel tends towards Jerusalem,
to which the journey narrative (9:51—19:27) is oriented.
The temptation to a messianic display in Jerusalem is rejected here, and in the event the true Messiah is revealed
in Jerusalem in his death and resurrection. The book of
Acts similarly narrates the proclamation of the gospel to
the world beginning from Jerusalem.

After a brief *introduction to the Galilean ministry (4:14-
15)* which summarizes the ministry rather than introduces
it, Luke places here *the rejection of Jesus at Nazareth
(4:16-30)*, which Mark and Matthew place nearer the close
of the Galilean ministry. Luke's account notably contains
material peculiar to himself; he abbreviates only the
criticisms of the Nazarenes, which is understood as a sign
of his delicacy. Only Luke gives the text (Isaiah 61:1-2) on

which Jesus gave his discourse. The text is associated with the Servant of the Lord passages, particularly Isaiah 42:1-4, and the identification of Jesus with the Servant was made in the early church. It was thus that a Messiah who was not a royal conqueror was explained. Only Luke has the proverb about the physician and the allusions to Elijah and Elisha, and he alone has the story of the threat on the life of Jesus. The climax suggests the powerful personality of Jesus rather than a miraculous escape.

The narrative of *a day at Capernaum (4:31-41)* follows Mark 1:21-34 rather closely, as does the *departure from Capernaum (4:42-44)*, except for two modifications: Luke does not mention Simon and his companions, since he places their call later, and he locates the subsequent preaching of Jesus in Judea. This is connected with Luke's Jerusalem theme. The call of the first disciples (5:1-11) is combined with the story of a marvelous catch of fish not related by Matthew and Mark. This justifies the saying about "catchers of men" (slightly altered from "fishers of men," Mark 1:17); the variation may be the occasion of the story of the catch. The self-abasing remark of Simon (5:8) is also peculiar to Luke, but it hardly reflects on Simon; here, Simon speaks for all the apostles and disciples. Andrew, Simon's brother, is strangely not mentioned by name, although he appears in the other three Gospels in the story of the call. *The cure of the leper (5:12-16)* also follows Mark 1:40-45 rather closely; but Luke strangely places the event "in a city," where it was most unlikely that a leper would appear; possibly this illustrates Luke's ignorance of Palestinian life. *The cure of the paralytic (5:17-26)* certainly illustrates this ignorance. Mark, who knew the dirt roofs of Palestinian houses, describes the digging of a hole in such a roof; these roofs can still be seen in Palestinian villages. Luke apparently had never seen such a roof; he took the story in good faith and added the incredible feat that the bearers of the sick man went through the tiles, scarcely less remarkable than the cure.

Luke follows Mark in *the call of Levi (5:27-32)*; like Mark, he is unaware of any identity of Levi with Matthew. The collection of *sayings associated with fasting (5:35-39)* is taken directly from Mark 2:18-22.

Luke's version of *the Sabbath controversy (6:1-5)* is abbreviated from Mark 2:23-28; both Luke and Matthew found Mark 2:27 too difficult to use. *The cure of the withered hand (6:6-11)* is likewise abbreviated by the omission of the references to the grief and anger of Jesus; in Luke Jesus begins to rise above human feeling. Luke alone prefaces *the call of the Twelve (6:12-16)* with the remark that Jesus spent the preceding night in prayer; this was an important decision not to be presented as if it had been made casually. Luke's list has one variation from Mark 3:16-19 and Matthew 10:2-4, the name of Judas son of Jacob instead of the Thaddaeus of Mark and Matthew. There is no explanation for this difference. Judas is mentioned elsewhere only by Luke in another list of the Eleven (Acts 1:13) and in John 14:22; but Thaddaeus does not appear outside the lists of Mark and Matthew.

The Infancy Narratives

Although Matthew and Luke both have infancy gospels, Mark and John do not. The simplest explanation for absence of the infancy in Mark is that he had no information. John, it seems, thought it more important to relate the eternal generation of the Word which became flesh. The question therefore is not why Mark does not have the infancy narrative, but why Matthew and Luke have it.

In the commentary we have given as much attention as possible to the problems raised by the variations between the two Gospels and with the known facts of external history. If this information is seriously considered, it will become clear that no simple harmonization is possible; the two cannot be reduced to a single source. If one is taken as original, the other is largely invented. In many ways Luke is the most picturesque of the Gospels in the sense that he has furnished more material for art than the other Gospels. The narrative of Luke has been painted so much that it has become familiar to all Christians even if they never look at the text. It is the Christian image; it has acquired a sacredness which makes the work of the historical critic seem to be almost a profanation.

Nevertheless, modern critics meet the problem not by saying that one of the Gospels is original and the other invented, but by saying that both are invented. There is not much reason for thinking that the childhood of Jesus was any better remembered than the childhood of any member of the poorer classes who achieved fame in adult life and after his death. In our own history we can mention Abraham Lincoln and even George Washington, who did not belong to the poorer classes; and both of these men were born in a time and a place where written records were much better kept than they were in Palestine of the first century. Details of the lives of famous men become interesting only after they have become famous; and when they have achieved fame, most of those who knew them as children are dead. In addition there is the universal tendency of popular narrative to see the future greatness of men foreshadowed in their childhood. New Testament writers like Mark and Paul do not show this interest; the gospel of Paul was that Jesus died for our sins and rose for our righteousness.

Many writers have borrowed a term for this type of imaginative narrative from Jewish literature; they call it *midrash,* which designates an imaginative expansion of a biblical passage. The infancy narratives are not properly midrash, in spite of a generous employment of Old Testament texts. There may indeed be no accurate literary definition of the infancy narratives. They are not simply fiction or wonder stories, since such designations take no account of their theological interest, which is serious. Nowhere else in the New Testament is the virgin birth, or rather the virginal conception, clearly stated; this belief may create problems, but certainly the infancy narratives have this statement as part of their purpose. It is one way of affirming that Jesus is the son of God. They also affirm that Jesus is Messiah and Lord. For Paul, Jesus was "designated" son of God in power by his resurrection (Romans 1:4), but this statement is earlier than the infancy narratives.

Let us return to our analogy. The birth of George Washington was not, strictly speaking, the birth of the Founder of his Country; it was the birth of a male infant to the Washingtons of Virginia. The event was fraught with historic significance, if you wish, but no one knew it. The artist or the writer who wishes to portray the event with its historic significance will have to use artistic symbolism. If the artist used the sometimes crude symbolism of less admired Christian artists, he might paint a stern-visaged infant standing in diapers in a boat full of Continental troops crossing the Delaware.

I have referred elsewhere to Christian artists as the best analogy of the infancy narratives. The symbolism which the Gospels created by words the artists portrayed in line and color. Both were attempting to portray the event in its full significance, and a simple birth scene does not show the significance. It needs hovering angels, worshiping poor, heavenly voices, an announcement like no other announcement, a light as unearthly as the skill of the artist, a picture of the meeting of God with his people, a picture of a unique event. Both the narratives and the paintings portray what is believed more than what is seen.

And since faith is a total personal conviction and not merely an assent to information, the artists and the Gospel meet the need to present what is believed with the vigor and color of life; they aim at the person, not at the mind. St. Ignatius Loyola urged those who contemplate the life of Jesus to enter the scene and to share the experience. He knew that the Gospels are eternally contemporary. But to enter the scene one must have a scene to enter; and if history does not furnish one, then the imagination can. Most Christians have been unable to read. When they could not, the church let them look at the pictures. Scholars too feel the need to look at the pictures, lest their faith degenerate from a total personal conviction to a mere intellectual persuasion.

Chapter Fourteen

THE GOSPEL OF LUKE, CHAPTERS 6–11

Sermon on the Plain

The introduction to the Sermon on the Plain (6:17-19) indicates great popular success; Luke is less explicit about rejection in Galilee than Mark is. The "plain" was not intended to stand in deliberate opposition to Matthew's "mountain" (Matthew 5:1); but Luke locates the discourse in a place accessible to people from distant points, suggesting the future spread of the missionary enterprise. Almost the entire *Sermon on the Plain (6:20-49)* is paralleled in Matthew, most of it in Matthew's Sermon on the Mount; this suggests that the discourse had been substantially compiled in Q. *The beatitudes (6:20-23)* of Luke number four, corresponding to the first, fourth and eighth of Matthew; Luke's third is close to Matthew's second, but not parallel. The "poor" in 6:20 is synonymous with Matthew's "poor in spirit" without the ambiguity which the English translation gives to Matthew. *The four woes (6:24-26)* are antithetical to the four beatitudes. The *sayings on love of one's enemies (6:27-35)* are parallel to Matthew 5:39-42+ 44-48; Luke has omitted some peculiarly Palestinian references and expanded on generosity in loans (6:34-35). The word "merciful" in 6:36 may reflect the source more faithfully than Matthew's (5:48) "perfect." *The sayings on compassion and integrity (6:36-45)* contain items found in Matthew both within and outside the Sermon on the Mount; the latter sayings appear to have had no context before the Gospels. The sayings in Luke are so arranged that they are addressed to the apostle rather than to Christians in general. *The parable of the true disciple (6:46-49)* is slightly altered; Luke did not catch the Palestinian allusions. Matthew thinks of a site which will not be washed away by rain, Luke of a deep foundation. In fact it is characteristic of Hellenistic sites in Palestine that the foundations are dug much more deeply than in any earlier constructions.

The cure of the centurion's servant (7:1-10) is modified from Matthew's version; Luke introduces Jews who intercede for the centurion, thus avoiding any personal encounter between Jesus and the centurion. The original points of the faith of the Gentile contrasted with Jewish unbelief and the healing at a distance solely by word are preserved, but Luke has added an atmosphere of good relations between Jews and Gentiles which probably represents an ideal rather than reality. *The raising of the son of the widow of Nain (7:11-17)* is peculiar to Luke. Jesus shows compassion for the poor and helpless. *The question of John the Baptist (7:18-35)* is close to Matthew 11:2-19. Luke has added a statement of fact in 7:21 to verify the quotation of Isaiah 35:5-6+61:1; and he has contrasted the popular belief in John with the unbelief of the Pharisees and the lawyers (7:29-30).

The Women in Luke

The story of the woman who was a sinner (7:36-50), insofar as it tells of a woman who anointed Jesus at dinner, is one of the few stories which is found in all four Gospels (Mark 14:3-9; Matthew 26:6-13, following Mark; John 12:1-8). The differences should be noticed. The other three evangelists place the incident before the passion. In Mark-Matthew the scene is Bethany and the host is Simon the leper; in John the woman is Mary of Bethany, the sister of Martha. In Mark and Matthew she anoints the head, commonly done at banquets; in Luke and John she anoints the feet, an unusual act in any hypothesis. This combination has led to an unjustified identification of Mary of Bethany with Mary Magdalen, a repentant prostitute. Luke has nothing in common with the other three. The point made in their stories is the extravagance of the woman's devotion to Jesus. In Luke the point is the love shown by the forgiven sinner, proportioned to the amount of sins forgiven. In fact it is proportioned to one's awareness of sinfulness, which is not determined by the rude quantity of one's sins. The *Jerusalem Bible* version of 7:47 removes a famous ambiguity in English versions which made the verse contradict itself.

The women who accompanied Jesus (8:1-3) are described only by Luke; he has more of an interest in women than the other evangelists. "The seven devils" of Mary Magdalen would more likely designate a disease than a life of sin. *The parable of the sower (8:4-15)* is abbreviated from Mark; Luke did not understand Palestinian farming very well. The harshness of Mark 4:10-12 is entirely removed, or possibly not really understood by Luke. *The parable of the lamp (8:16-18)* is a strange combination of sayings found in other contexts in Mark and Matthew; Luke refers them to the proclamation of the full gospel to the Gentiles and the rejection of the unbelieving Jews. Here Luke places *the saying about the mother and brothers of Jesus (8:19-21);* they become examples of the preceding saying, and the embarrassment of Mark 3:31-35 is entirely removed.

The calming of the storm (8:22-25) is abbreviated from Mark, as is *the cure of the daughter of Jairus and of the woman with a hemorrhage (8:40-56).* In both passages Luke abbreviates less sharply than Matthew, but both Matthew and Luke show little interest in the picturesque details of Mark. *The sending of the Twelve (9:1-6)* follows Mark; but Luke 9:2, and only Luke, describes the mission much as it is described in Acts. *The remark of Herod (9:7-9)* is reported according to Mark. *The feeding of the five thousand (9:10-17)* is only slightly abbreviated from

Mark; Luke, who avoids even the appearance of duplication, does not have the feeding of the four thousand. *The
confession of Peter (9:18-21)* does not have the emphasis
it has in Mark and Matthew; and *the first prediction of the
passion (9:22)* omits the protest of Peter and the rebuke of
Jesus. Thus *the sayings about the conditions of discipleship (9:23-27)* lose some of the sharpness which the context
in Mark and Matthew gives them. As in Mark and Matthew, *the transfiguration (9:28-36)*, related according to
Mark, furnishes the promise of glory as a background for
the prediction of the passion. Luke omits the question
about Elijah (Mark 9:9-13) and the identification of Elijah
with John the Baptist (Matthew 17:9-13). *The cure of the
epileptic (9:37-43)* is notably abbreviated from Mark; of
interest is the question of the disciples and their powerless-
ness due to lack of faith; Luke found this too offensive to
use. *The second prediction of the passion (9:44-45)* retains
from Mark one of Luke's rare allusions to the failure of the
disciples to understand. The *saying about the child (9:46-
48)*, as in Mark, is directed to kindness toward the weak;
only Matthew 18:1-5 has referred the saying to the dispute
about comparative greatness, unquestionably the original
reference. *The saying about exorcism in the name of Jesus
(9:49-50)*, as in Mark, extols the power of the name of
Jesus, a theme which Luke emphasizes in the early chapters of Acts. The concluding saying is in paradoxical
opposition to 11:23.

The episode of the Samaritan village (9:51-56), peculiar
to Luke, begins a new section with a rejection of Jesus, as
the rejection at Nazareth began the public life in Luke.
Later a Samaritan appears as a model of the virtue which
this village denies. In his response, Jesus declines to use
his miraculous power for destruction; rather he admits to
rudeness. This episode begins the narrative of the journey
to Jerusalem. *The sayings about discipleship (9:57-62)* emphasize the urgency of the call. They parallel Matthew
8:19-22, but Luke has a third saying of his own. Only Luke

has *the mission of the seventy or seventy-two disciples (10:1-16);* the number may echo the seventy elders appointed by Moses (Numbers 11:16). The instructions are parallel to the instructions of the Twelve in Matthew 10: 7-16; Luke describes the larger missionary effort of the church as initiated by Jesus himself, but the mission of Jesus is directed only to Jews. Luke has added here the saying about the unbelief of the cities on the shore of the Sea of Galilee, which in Matthew more clearly implies the failure of the mission in Galilee. *The saying about the privilege of the disciples (10:23-24)* is given in a context different from the context in Matthew; originally tho saying stood isolated.

The Lord's Prayer

The question of the lawyer (10:25-28) is not put in the rabbinical form concerning the greatest commandment of the Law; possibly Luke did not understand this way of putting the question. Only Luke has the lawyer's further question answered by the parable of the Good Samaritan (10:29-37). This interpretation of the first commandment, which the church has never accepted quite completely, must have arisen in answer to questions raised in the early church when its membership expanded beyond a single ethnic group. The community of "neighbors" is not formed by ethnic unity but by the exchange of the services of neighborliness without respect to ethnic divisions (see Galatians 3:28). *The story of Martha and Mary (10:38-42)* is often regarded as unfair to Mary and to her concerns: she also heard the words of Jesus, and Luke elsewhere (8:1-3) praises the women who ministered to the needs of Jesus. But the saying without the story is close to 12:22-31 (Q) from which it may be derived. Luke's version of *the Lord's Prayer (11:1-4)* contains another reference to the prayer of Jesus which is peculiar to Luke. The prayer has five petitions against Matthew's seven; neither is "origi-

nal," but both come from different liturgical traditions of
the early church. The theme of prayer is expanded in *the
parable of the importunate friend (11:5-8),* peculiar to Luke;
it is more easily understood if one realizes that ancient
locks and bars made the closing and opening of the house a
major operation each night and morning. *Further sayings
about prayer (11:9-13)* are parallel to Matthew.

In the *dispute about Beelzebul (11:14-22),* Luke agrees
with Matthew rather than with Mark; this indicates that
this story was found both in Mark and in Q. Luke omits
the difficult sayings of Matthew 12:31-32 and Mark 3:28-
29. The sayings which follow occur in the same context as
in Matthew, but the order is altered. *The return of the evil
spirit (11:24-26)* is close to Matthew's version; it stands
here by association with Beelzebul. *The blessing of the
mother of Jesus (11:27-28)* is peculiar to Luke; it is similar
to the saying about true kinship with Jesus (8:19-21). *The
sign of Jonah (11:29-32)* is shorter than Matthew 12:38-42,
but the abbreviation occurs only in the references to Jonah;
the Gentile Luke retained the entire references to the
Ninevites and the queen of the south, all believing Gentiles.
The sayings about the lamp (11:33-36) combine sayings
scattered in Matthew; they are joined by verbal association. *The discourse against the Pharisees and the lawyers
(11:37-54)* contains nothing which is not found in Matthew
23; but Luke is briefer, he locates the discourse at a dinner
given by a Pharisee, makes the unspoken criticism of the
Pharisee the occasion of the discourse, and distinguishes
between the Pharisees and the lawyers (called scribes by
the other evangelists). The community of Matthew and
Luke suggests that Q had sayings about scribes and Pharisees already grouped into a discourse.

Abbreviations in Luke

The reader of this portion of the commentary is bound to
feel both bored and disappointed at too frequently repeated
remarks like "Luke abbreviates. . . ." We ought to meet his

disappointment by dwelling at least briefly on the significance of these apparently idle remarks. By comparing one
Gospel with others we can come to a good insight on what
the writer was and what he thought he was doing. And
these abbreviations show what tradition has always maintained that Luke was a Gentile, unacquainted with Palestine, uninformed about Judaism, not understanding it very
well and a little afraid of it.

In so describing Luke I am aware that I am describing
most contemporary Christians. We ought to be sympathetic with Luke because he has some of our problems. I
said, for instance, that he did not understand Judaism very
well. In the commentary the reader will notice frequently
enough that Luke omits something for the alleged reason
that he did not understand what it meant. Such comments
are found where the other Gospels use some Jewish expression or refer to some Jewish practice. Luke did not
explain these things because he could not. He represents
most of the early Gentile church, which heard the Jewish
background of the proclamation and missed most of it.
Unconsciously they replaced the Jewish background with
a Hellenistic background. The Greek word which we translate "savior" was not a Jewish messianic title; it was a
word applied to Hellenistic gods and Hellenistic kings.
Many writers say that it sums up Luke's presentation of
the mission of Jesus. It was an effort to make the unintelligible Jewish word *messiah* (in Greek, *christos*) meaningful to those who were called to believe that Jesus is
Messiah and Lord. It was an accurate translation, but it
was a translation. The Hellenistic savior was primarily a
healer; when Jesus is given the title it refers to his healing
of disease and of sin.

The reader will be more disturbed when he reads that
Luke omitted something because he found it too harsh.
This comment appears in reference to such things as the
failure of the disciples to understand, ill feeling between
Jews and Gentiles, and even some extremely concrete

expressions about the renunciation which Jesus demands.
All this put together could indicate that Luke intended to
produce a bland mixture which would excite no one. This
is not a good description of Luke's Gospel, but to say this
does not solve the problem of his extraordinary freedom
towards his sources. Certainly if he thought that Mark and
Q gave him "the exact words" of Jesus, he felt free to re-
write them in the direction of blandness. He could not
have thought the words were sacred. More probably he
recognized better than Matthew and Mark that Aramaic
translated into Greek had a roughness and a directness
which was displeasing to the educated Greek ear. In English "shut up" and "please be quiet" ask the same thing,
but they cannot be used interchangeably. At the same time,
to tamper with the rough directness of popular speech
risks losing some of its peculiar force. This may not explain
all of Luke's blandness, but it is probably the best single
explanation. We assume that sometimes he produced
blandness without intending it.

This does not explain such things as his treatment of the
disciples, the words of Jesus about his mother and kinsmen
and some ethnic allusions about Jews and Gentiles; and I
see no explanation for this except that Luke here acted as
a censor of the news. Such apparently scandalous sayings
would do his readers no good, he thought. He was a peacemaker; this can clearly be seen in the book of Acts. In the
church of Luke every one loves every one else; those in
authority are fully responsible and aware that they are
servants and those who are governed are docile and
charitable. Luke did not wash the family linen in public.
Were it not for some other New Testament books, we
would not know that there was any family linen. Ultimately this means that both in the Gospel and in Acts
Luke presents the picture of what the church ought to be
much more clearly than he presents the picture of what it
was.

Another feature of Luke's abbreviation is his omission of

the graphic details of Mark, which we see in Matthew also. This does not seem quite in accord with what I said earlier, that Luke is the most picturesque of the Gospels. He is, in his own material, but where Mark is already picturesque Luke abbreviates almost as if he were not interested and wished to hurry on to his own contributions. There is, however, another factor at work. In Matthew and Luke the slow transformation from the earthy Jesus of Mark to the unearthly Jesus of John is in process. Luke's omissions, like Matthew's, create an atmosphere of serenity, of complete control, of mastery of oneself and of others and of events which rests on an assurance of unearthly resources of power. As Luke viewed his material, Jesus is Lord, and it should not be thought that he was pretending to be something else. When Luke's abbreviations of Mark are compared with the material peculiar to Luke, it will be seen that the same transcendent Jesus appears in both.

Chapter Fifteen

THE GOSPEL OF
LUKE, CHAPTERS 12–19

Open and Fearless Speech

In the saying about the leaven of the Pharisees (12:1-2), found in Matthew and Mark, only Luke explains the leaven as hypocrisy; the easiest explanation in Matthew and Mark is that it signifies doctrine. *The sayings about open and fearless confession (12:3-12)* are found in Matthew 10:19, 26-33, except for the saying about the word against the Son of Man, which is included here purely by verbal association. In both Gospels, the sayings not only reflect the persecutions of the early Church but also face the danger of apostasy. *The sayings about possessions (12:13-21),* peculiar to Luke, show Luke's emphasis upon renunciation of worldly goods. The refusal of Jesus to arbitrate a dispute about possessions is one of the most extreme denials of interest in wealth in all the Gospels. The rich fool is condemned not for ordinary prudence and foresight, but implicitly for not giving his abundance to the poor. *The sayings on trust in Providence (12:22-32)* are placed here by topical association and are found also in Matthew 6:19-33. This rejection of foresight goes beyond the parable of the rich fool; Luke softens somewhat the rigor of the saying by the promise of the kingdom (12:32), peculiar to himself. *The saying about almsgiving (12:33-34)* follows more logically the sayings about trust. *The saying about the faithful steward (12:35-48)* comes from the Q (see Matthew 24:43-51); it is directed to the officers of the Church and in particular to those who have lost sight of the Second

Coming. *Sayings about Jesus (12:49-53)* look to his future
in suffering and to the decision which he imposes upon
those who encounter him. *Sayings about the times (12:54-
58)* state the imminence of the decision and its finality. The
urgency of changing one's life is stated in the saying about
repentance (13:1-5); no one can escape the decision. *The
parable of the barren fig tree (13:6-9)* continues the theme
of the necessity of decision; it is probable that this parable
has become an incident in Matthew and Mark. *The healing
of the crippled woman (13:10-17)* is peculiar to Luke; however, the primacy of helping the neighbor over the precept
of Sabbath observance is familiar in all the Gospels. *The
parables of the mustard seed and the leaven (13:18-21)* are
found in Mark (4:30-32) and Matthew (13:31-32); Luke
adds nothing of his own. *The sayings about the door (13:
22-30)*, scattered in Matthew, are brought together here by
association (door, exclusion). The collection is so organ-
ized that the sayings are all directed to the exclusion of
the Jews from the reign. *The saying about Herod the fox
(13:31-33)* is peculiar to Luke; it affirms the foreknowledge
of Jesus and his destiny at Jerusalem. *The lament over
Jerusalem (13:34-35)* is placed here by verbal association.

  The healing of the man with dropsy (14:1-6) is very
similar to Luke 6:6-11 (Matthew 12:9-14, and Mark 3:1-6);
Luke places the saying about the primacy of charity here.
The sayings against vanity (14:7-14) are peculiar to Luke,
but the saying of 14:11 is repeated in 18:14 (Matthew 23:
12). The motivation seems rather low, but the sayings are
uttered in irony. The man who seeks vain esteem takes
steps which will surely lose it. By verbal association, the
saying about generosity to those who cannot repay is
placed here (14:12-14); peculiar to Luke, this is a striking
statement of the duty of almsgiving without any self-
interest. By continued association there follows *the parable
of the great supper (14:15-24)*. Luke's version, which lacks
the difficulties of Matthew 22:1-10, is probably closer to
the original form. The point that the Jews reject the invita-

tion, which is then extended to the Gentiles, remains the same in both versions. *The sayings on discipleship (14:25-35)*, except for 14:25-27, 34-35, are peculiar to Luke; they exhibit Luke's emphasis on total renunciation, and warn the prospective disciples not to make the decision hastily. The invitation is extended to all, but its terms must not be minimized.

Three "parables of mercy" follow, one of which, the parable of the lost sheep, is paralleled in Matthew 18:12-14. The situation (15:1-2) is roughly parallel to Luke 5:29-30 (Matthew 9:10-11, Mark 2:15-16). Luke's sympathy with the poor leads him to accept the Pharisaic identification of the poor with sinners for the sake of the argument. The theme of the first two parables is the search for sinners; the theme of the third is the readiness to receive the repenter. *The parable of "the prodigal son" is more correctly the parable of "the two brothers";* the readiness of God to receive the repentant sinner is contrasted with the harsh and unforgiving disposition of the righteous, easily identified as the Pharisees. The "sinners" are not obviously Gentiles; they also include the poor and the nonobservant Jews.

The parable of the crafty steward (16:1-8), peculiar to Luke, is difficult for many readers; the steward is praised for his foresight, not for his dishonesty. The contrast between dishonesty and foresight is paradoxical; the honest sometimes fail in that virtue which the dishonest manifest. There follow, by association, *some sayings on the use of money (16:9-13)*, also peculiar to Luke. The right use of money can only be almsgiving; the saying reflects the popular belief that all wealth is tainted. *The saying about the Pharisees (16:14-15)*, associated with the preceding by the rather gratuitous remark that the Pharisees loved money, is a charge of hypocrisy, not of avarice. *The sayings about the Law (16:16-18)* have in common only that they deal in some way with the Law; they are from Q, found in scattered contexts in Matthew. Luke probably

did not understand the difficult saying about violence
(Matthew 11:12) and abbreviated it. *The parable of the
rich man and Lazarus (16:19-31)*, peculiar to Luke, is a
severe indictment of the indifference of the rich. The rich
man does nothing and for that he is punished; he is not
positively cruel and merciless, he is simply insensitive. The
passage reflects popular Jewish ideas about the world to
come; the concluding line may allude to the refusal of the
Jews to believe in the resurrection of Jesus.

The Disciples' Duties

The collection of sayings (17:1-10) has no common theme
except that they deal with the duties of the disciples; and
the parable of the unprofitable servants indicates that
these sayings are directed to the ministry of the disciples.
Except for the parable, peculiar to Luke, they are Q sayings found in scattered contexts in Matthew. They deal
with the avoidance of scandal (the "little ones" mean not
children, but the simple), the duty of forgiveness (rather
than the duty of correction), and the growth of faith. The
parable of the unprofitable servants announces that the
ministry is a task which is never fully done; total dedication is merely the minimum of fulfillment. *The healing of
the ten lepers (17:11-19)*, peculiar to Luke, contrasts the
gratitude of the Samaritan with the ingratitude of the Jews;
it is typical of the whole proclamation of the Gospel. *The
saying about the kingdom (17:20-21)* poses a still unsolved difficulty; "within you" can mean "already present"
(in Jesus) or "within your grasp" (by faith in the gospel).
The discourse on the day of the Son of Man (17:22-37) is
parallel to part of the eschatological discourse of Matthew
and to Luke 21:25-28; Luke distinguishes more clearly than
Mark and Matthew between the coming of the Son of
Man and the destruction of Jerusalem, already an event of
the past when Luke wrote. The discourse warns that the
coming of the Son of Man is later than was expected, and
that when he does come, it will be sudden and unexpected.
There will be no time for a quick change of heart.

The parable of the unscrupulous judge (18:1-8) is peculiar to Luke. As the parable of the crafty steward makes an immoral person the model of a virtue, so this parable makes an immoral person an example of the behavior of God. The final sentence has no connection either with what precedes or with what follows. *The parable of the Pharisee and the publican (18:9-14),* also peculiar to Luke, carries on the theme of the difference between the self-righteous and the repentant sinner. The candid picture of the self-righteous man is impressive in its simplicity. *The blessing of the children (18:15-17)* follows Mark (10:13-16) verbally, except for the mention of the anger of Jesus, which Luke omits. *The story of the rich man (18:18-30;* a "young man" only in Matthew) is abbreviated from Mark by the omission of some repetitions in the words of the disciples concerning renunciation and its rewards. *The third prediction of the passion (18:31-34)* follows Mark closely; however it is more detailed than the earlier predictions. Strangely, only Luke includes the emphatic denial that the disciples understood the prediction. Some commentators suggest that it associates the disciples' spiritual blindness with the physical blindness of which the man of Jericho was cured (18:35-43). This episode is taken from Mark (10:46-52) with the omission of descriptive details, in particular the words exchanged between the blind man and some of the crowd.

The Story of Zacchaeus

The episode of Zacchaeus (19:1-10) is peculiar to Luke. It exhibits the Lucan theme of the openness of Jesus to "sinners"—Jews whose profession or condition of life made them outcasts to the Pharisees. To such, Jesus extends a special invitation, and it is received with grateful repentance. These, the conclusion implies, are more genuine "sons of Abraham" than the self-righteous Pharisees. *The parable of the pounds (19:11-27),* if the references to receiving a kingdom and punishing the enemies are omitted, appears to be Q material paralleled in Matthew 25:14-30. Luke, by his addition, applies the parable more directly to the disciples who administer the Church, the estate of Jesus. The kingdom is not in the immediate future; they must do their duty in order to gain admission. The administration of the Church must show expansion by the admission of new believers; the one who buries his pound in a napkin represents the Jewish people who make no effort to spread the kingdom to the Gentiles. Jesus goes to receive his kingdom in his ascension; those who do not recognize his kingship—again the Jews—will be punished. The details of receiving the kingship have a striking resemblance to the succession of Archelaus to Herod's kingdom; the Jews sent a delegation to protest his succession. Archelaus, however, was deposed a few years later by Augustus.

Exclusively in Luke

In the introduction to Luke we mentioned Luke's account of the journey to Jerusalem (9:51—19:27), which is much longer than the parallel accounts in Mark and Matthew. Luke has expanded the narrative by the inclusion of material peculiar to himself. Earlier I spoke of the impression one occasionally has of Luke hurrying through the material of Mark to get to his own contributions. The impression is probably too imaginative for sober interpretation; the fact remains that out of 1150 verses Luke has 500-600 without parallel in the other two Gospels. Clearly he had new material, and the presumption is that he knew it. It is this new material which keeps Luke from being the bland mixture suggested earlier; and it will repay us to survey his major themes.

The theme that Jesus was a friend of sinners is common to the three Synoptic Gospels (Matthew 9:11 and 11:18-19; Mark 2:16). Luke not only has parallels to these passages, but he expands the theme by his own material, which includes some of the best known and most often quoted passages of the Gospels. Thus his treatment of the barren fig tree (13:6-9) is so different from the fig tree of Matthew 21:18-19 and Mark 11:13-14 that we wonder whether we have the same saying at all. The parables of Luke 15 include the lost sheep, the lost drachma and the prodigal son, all classic expressions of the search of God for the sinner. The sinful woman (7:36-50) is an extended affirmation of the mercy of Jesus to prostitutes; see Matthew 21:32. The tax collector was the paradigmatic "sinner" of first century Palestinian Judaism; Zacchaeus hears the call of Jesus and alters his manner of life, in obvious contrast to the Pharisees. The same theme is repeated in the parable of the Pharisee and the tax collector (18:10-14). Possibly the greatest expression of mercy in Luke is the words to the repentant bandit on the cross (23:40-43). It is evident that much preaching on mercy and forgiveness would have been impoverished without this Lucan material; and it may be worth noting again that in most of these parables Luke has a narrative which can be painted.

The theme of mercy to sinners goes farther than the surface shows. To Jews, all Gentiles were sinners by definition. St. Francis Xavier in one of his letters relates his encounter with the Chinese captain of a ship on which he sailed. Although they could not converse, Xavier expresses his admiration of the captain's nobility and good manners, and his regret that the captain is going to hell. This almost incredible sixteenth century narrowness was what drove Xavier to the missionary field; at the same time he spoke for the Judaism of the first century rather than for the Gospels. Luke must have been put in his place often by Jewish Christians, for he cheerfully accepts the identification of Gentiles with sinners; they are the lost whom Jesus came to seek and save (19:10). He introduces Samaritans as models of charity (10:25-37) and of gratitude (17:11-19) and Gentiles as models of good conduct and ready faith (7:9). Mark, who wrote for Gentiles, had not felt the sting of Jewish superiority as Luke had. Possibly Luke's recognized interest in women reflects his Hellenism; the social and legal position of women was higher in Hellenism than it was in Judaism, and Luke probably meant to show that the Judaism of the Gospel did not include the Jewish attitude towards women.

No interpreter has ever failed to note that Luke is preeminently the Gospel of the poor and of poverty, and one need only draw the attention of the reader to this; a careful and reflective reading of the Gospel will disclose this theme in all its fullness. Luke's peculiar material on giving to the poor includes such well-known passages as the parables of Dives and Lazarus (16:19-31) and the rich fool (12:13-21) and the recommendation to invite the poor to the banquet (14:12-14), a recommendation which made as much sense in the social world of Hellenism as it does in our own. The two parables have a penetrating edge; the two men are condemned for not doing anything. Where compassion to the poor and the helpless is concerned Luke is in no way bland.

Neither is he bland when he speaks of the renunciation which Jesus demands of the disciples. In 14:26,33 Luke achieves a harshness which is not found in Matthew 10:37. By slight modifications in such renunciation passages as 5:11,28; 11:41; 12:13-33; 14:26,33; 18:29 Luke somewhat subtly introduces an emphasis on "all"; the renunciation which Jesus demands is total. One cannot help wondering whether these subtle modifications do not come from an experience of renunciation, either of Luke himself or of those whom he knew, which was not shared by the authors of Matthew and Mark.

These observations may help to show that Luke, when he interpreted the gospel as a Gentile for Gentiles, bewildered as he was sometimes by the language and the culture of Palestinian Judaism, did interpret it without diluting it. Not all Gentiles have been so successful.

Chapter Sixteen

THE GOSPEL OF
LUKE, CHAPTERS 19-24

Last Days in Jerusalem

In the account of *the entrance of Jesus into Jerusalem (19:28-40)* Luke follows Mark rather closely. But only Luke has the saying about the stones (19:39-40); the coming of the Messiah to Jerusalem is an event which must be announced, even if a marvel is necessay to do it. *The saying about the fall of Jerusalem (19:41-44)* is peculiar to Luke, who distinguishes more clearly than Matthew and Mark between the fall of Jerusalem and the end-catastrophe. Luke, like Matthew, wrote after the fall of Jerusalem in 70 A.D.; he alludes to the Roman siege technique of *circumvallatio,* the erection of an earthwork embankment which prevented access to the besieged city and egress from it. The cleansing of the temple is slightly abbreviated from Mark; it is surprising that Luke omits "for the Gentiles" (Isaiah 56:7) in 45, since this phrase contributes to his interest in the Gentiles.

The question of the authority of Jesus (20:1-8) is treated according to Mark. Luke's rewriting of *the parable of the wicked husbandmen (20:9-19)* is small but significant. Of all the messengers only the son is killed; and before the son is killed he is cast out of the vineyard. This clearly signifies that Judaism has rejected Jesus, and Luke thus emphasizes the polemical character of the parable as Mark and Matthew do not. *The question of the tribute to Caesar (20:20-26)* is handled according to Mark; but Luke is much more explicit about the malicious purpose of the question, and clearly implies that the question failed in its purpose. *The question about the resurrection (20:27-40)* is also treated according to Mark, but Luke's small additions raise a major theological problem; for in 35-36 Luke makes it clear that the answer deals only with the resurrection of the righteous. *The question of the Son of David (20:41-44)*, which must have had little significance for the Gentile Luke, is abbreviated to the minimum. *The sayings against the scribes (20:45-47)* are very brief here; see also 11:39-51. Luke preserves little of the bitterness of Jewish-Christian controversy which appears in Mark and Matthew. *The story of the widow's mite (21:1-4)* is abbreviated from Mark; Luke, in spite of his interest in the poor, saw nothing here of special interest. He places it, however, by the catchword "widow" in contrast with the preceding saying about the scribes.

Luke's version of *the apocalyptic discourse (21:5-36)* is entirely paralleled in Mark (13:1-37), but Luke has edited the material somewhat in order to bring out some of his own theological points. The *introduction (21:5-7)* is a prediction of the destruction of Jerusalem and a question about the time of this event. *The answer about the signs (21:8-19)* is less clearly eschatological than Mark (13:5-13); but the events in nature (8-11) lie beyond the contemporary scene, as indicated in 12. The persecutions announced by Jesus had already occurred. *The destruction of Jerusalem (21:20-24)* was an event of the past when Luke wrote; but the coming of the Son of Man had not followed this event. It introduced "the age of the pagans" (21:24), which would endure until the Second Coming. *The signs of the Second Coming (21:25-28)* were natural convulsions which had not yet occurred. Thus Luke was able to retain *the parable of the fig tree and the announcement of the Parousia (21:29-33)*; but the scope of the prediction becomes much less definite by the omission of "these things" in Mark's phrase "all these things"; Luke makes it a prediction of the entire history of salvation. *The warning to be alert (21:34-36)* is peculiar to Luke in this form; that the Parousia is remote does not permit the believer to act as if it had no relevance to himself. *The summary of the teaching of Jesus in Jerusalem (21:37-38)* links the discourse with the passion narrative proper, which follows.

Luke's version of the Passion has a number of passages peculiar to Luke. *The conspiracy and the betrayal (22:1-6)* are taken from Mark in 1-2, but Luke strangely expands Mark in 3-6 regarding the betrayal. The expansion is purely rhetorical, adding nothing to the details. *The preparation for the Passover (22:7-13)* follows Mark, except that Peter and John are namcd as the messengers; this is peculiar to Luke. *The account of the institution of the Eucharist (22:14-20)* contains a problem which is at once textual, exegetical and theological. The traditional text has two cups. Some ancient MSS have only one, the first, which is contrary to the traditional order and lacks the Eucharistic formula. There is no certain solution to the problem, but most modern scholars believe the longer text is the original. Luke placed *the prediction of the betrayal (22:21-23)* after the institution, not before as in Mark (14:17-21) and Matthew (26:20-25); at this time "the hands" of all were on the table, and the rearrangement is probably a subtle warning against treachery within the established community. Hence the location here of *the saying about greatness (22: 24-27)*, transferred from its context in Mark, is not merely by chance; the temptation to greatness is a major temptation to betrayal. *The promise of a reward (22:28-30)* assumes that the group addressed has successfully overcome the temptation. *The prediction of Peter's denial (22:31-34)* contains a Lucan expansion. The emphasis is placed less upon the fall than upon Peter's recovery; and Luke's statement of the pre-eminence of Peter among the Twelve is associated with his ascendancy after his denial. *The saying about the two swords (22:35-38)* is peculiar to Luke; not only the entire Gospel tradition, but also the Lucan form of that tradition, impose the interpretation of the saying

as a figurative warning to prepare for attack; see Matthew
26:52. *The account of Gethsemane (22:39-46)* is sharply
abbreviated from Mark, and in particular no emotional dis-
turbance is attributed to Jesus. Hence the omission of 43-44
in the most ancient and important MSS is very probably
original; these verses may be a scribal expansion adding
the features which the reader missed in Luke. Luke's account of *the arrest of Jesus (22:47-53)* omits the kiss of
Judas, possibly from delicacy. He, with John, notes that
the right ear of the servant was cut off—which suggests
unusual clumsiness in a right-handed swordsman; and
Luke alone mentions the instant cure of the wound. He
omits the explicit note that the disciples abandoned Jesus;
but he retains a form of the saying which shows that Jesus
is master of the events. Luke has no nocturnal process before the council, but *the denial of Peter (22:54-62)* occurs
at night in the house of the high priest. Luke has synthe-
sized the narrative, mentioning three different inquirers,
omitting the cursing and swearing of Peter, and adding his
own visual touch of the direct gaze of Jesus directed at
Peter while he denied Jesus. Luke, like most modern interpreters, must have found the two sessions of the council
confusing; he simply omitted the night session and retained only the account of *the mocking of Jesus (22:63-65)*.

Passion and Death

The trial before the Sanhedrin (22:66-71) is abbreviated
from Mark. For Luke the legal charge against Jesus is no
longer of any importance; he was crucified for being Messiah and Son of God. It seems that for Luke the attitude
of the Roman governor was of more importance. In *the
first hearing before Pilate (23:1-7)* Jesus is declared innocent of the claim to kingship. *The remanding of the case
to Herod (23:8-12)* is peculiar to Luke, and it is historically
doubtful; but it is another affirmation by a legal authority
that Jesus, while he may be ridiculous, is innocent of any
crime. *The second hearing before Pilate (23:13-25)* is nar-

rated in such a way that Pilate clearly yielded to pressure from "the chief priests, the leading men and the people." The reference to the obligation of freeing a prisoner on the Passover (23:17) is not found in the most important witnesses. Luke has no reference to the scourging—very probably from delicacy again; and he implies in 23:25 that Jesus was executed by the Jews. The story of *the way to Calvary (23:26-32)* is expanded in Luke by the encounter of Jesus with the women of Jerusalem; this is an explicit reference to the coming destruction of the city. In the account of *the crucifixion (23:33-34)* the prayer of Jesus for forgiveness, peculiar to Luke, is missing in a large number of important ancient MSS; the verse must be regarded as doubtful. In *the mocking of Jesus (23:35-38)* Luke distinguishes between the speech of the leaders and the silence of the people. *The episode of the thieves (23:39-43)* is peculiar to Luke; the repentant sinner is saved at the last possible moment, and salvation was equally available to both. The words of Jesus imply his instant glorification; this is not entirely in accord with Luke's theology of the resurrection and the ascension. *The last words of Jesus (23:44-46)* are peculiar to Luke; they again exhibit the mastery of Jesus over events, even over his own death. Luke omits Mark's (15:34) cry of abandonment; it suggests human weakness. *The centurion's profession of faith (23: 47-49)* is changed by Luke from Mark's "son of God" to "a righteous (innocent) man." The account of *the burial (23:50-56)* depends on Mark; Luke, however, explicitly excuses Joseph from any part in the condemnation of Jesus (v. 51a), and adds 23:55-56 in preparation for the following narrative. Otherwise he sharply abbreviates.

The account of the resurrection (24:1-11) depends on Mark 16:1-8; Luke has two men instead of Mark's one, and he says more explicitly that the women did not find the body of Jesus. According to Luke's theory of the resurrection appearances there is no mention of a proposed meeting in Galilee; it is interesting that Luke retains the word

"Galilee." Luke and John say that the women announced the empty tomb to the disciples; Mark and Matthew include the commission but not the execution. The unbelief of the disciples is emphasized in Luke's resurrection narratives. Luke 24:12 reflects John 20:6, and is missing in the most important MSS.

The story of the disciples at Emmaus (24:13-35) is peculiar to Luke; and the numerous historical problems which it raises suggest an early symbolic narrative. The presence of the risen Jesus in the Eucharist is affirmed; there he is recognized as ever present in the community. Furthermore, the Scriptural proclamation of the redeeming death as recognized in the Eucharist reveals its significance and confirms faith in his death and resurrection. Emmaus cannot be definitely located. *The apparition of Jesus to the apostles (24:36-43)* again emphasizes their slowness to believe; a demonstration of the three-dimensional reality of the risen body (not the two-dimensional "ghost") is given by eating. The explanation of the redeeming death and resurrection is again based on the Scriptures; Jesus is the initiator of the apostolic catechesis. *The ascension (24: 50-53)* is a theological theory peculiar to Luke in the New Testament. Other writers imply that the glorification of Jesus begins with the resurrection. The repetition of the narrative in Acts joins together the two books of Luke.

Textual Problems

Part IV of Luke contains three interesting textual problems, and some slightly more extended treatment of the methods involved in handling such problems is in order. In 22:17-20 there are two cups, one before and one after the bread; some of the earliest manuscripts omit the second cup. In 22:43-44 the bloody sweat is not found in the most ancient manuscripts. In 23:34 the prayer of Jesus for the forgiveness of his executioners is omitted by some of the major manuscripts.

The Gospels have come to us in more than 2500 manuscripts which antedate the invention of printing. The more recent manuscripts are copied from older manuscripts, and consequently the older manuscripts are normally closer to the original. But the problem is much more complex than that. More recent manuscripts may be copies of better manuscripts now lost; older manuscripts may have been bad copies. The science of textual criticism consists in laborious comparison of the manuscripts with the purpose of arriving at a judgment as to which of the manuscripts are least altered from the original. The manuscripts which meet the tests are the manuscripts which give us the Gospels; conversely, in the three cases mentioned most of these (and for the bloody sweat all of them) do not give us the verses in question. The critic must then ask whence they come; that is, whether the recent manuscripts may not have something which the older and better manuscripts lost.

When a verse is added or omitted, the critic must look for tendentiousness in the editor; can he think of a reason why the editor may have deliberately expanded or shortened the text he received? The three passages in question illustrate this principle, although the principle does not furnish a certain answer. Thus the order of bread-wine is established for the earliest liturgies of the Eucharist. It is impossible that Luke should have inverted this order; therefore the second cup must belong to the original text. Hence the received text must be preferred, in spite of the difficulty that the Gentile Luke alludes to a part of the Passover ritual which we would not expect him to know. Furthermore, some scribes must have confused the first clearly non-Eucharistic cup with the second. But this is the least difficult assumption.

For the bloody sweat, peculiar to Luke, one must observe that Luke never attributes the external expression of strong feeling to Jesus. Outside of these verses he does not attribute strong feeling to Jesus in this prayer, as Mark

does. Since the manuscripts deny us this verse and its
omission is in harmony with Luke's patterns of thought,
the probabilities are all against it. In addition we may cite
Luke's delicacy, often mentioned as a reason for omission
—the scourging, for instance. If Luke wrote here according
to his habits, he would omit the bloody sweat even if his
sources gave it to him. Rarely do the manuscript evidence
and the literary assumptions meet so nicely as they do in
this passage. But the critic finds it difficult to explain the
source; and since it is a general principle that a line which
departs from the expected patterns of the writer is pre-
sumed to be original, the conclusion retains a degree of
doubt. Behind this principle is the principle that editors
tend to correct the unusual, not the usual.

The prayer for forgiveness is also peculiar to Luke, but,
contrary to the bloody sweat, it is entirely in accord with
Luke's patterns of thought; Luke is the Gospel of mercy.
Furthermore, Luke rather obviously does not lay the blame
for the death of Jesus very heavily on any one, either Jews
or Romans; he remains the peacemaker even in that part
of the narrative where peacemaking appears impossible.
Yet most of the manuscripts which are the sources of the
text deny us this verse. We said that the critic must look
for tendentiousness. Possibly in this verse we may find it.
In the early centuries, when Christian-Jewish controversies
had become embittered and Christians were often persecuted by Roman authorities and Roman mobs, it is con-
ceivable that some vindictive scribes exercised such
freedom with the sacred text. In the first place, we do not
know that he recognized it as sacred. In the second place,
the ancient scribe seemed to regard himself as a kind of
author-editor. In the third place, those who worry about
this should be reminded of the remark of Hort, a famous
tex.ual critic of the nineteenth century, that seven-eighths
of the text of the New Testament is above suspicion. No
other work from ancient times approaches this degree of
fidelity in transmission. For this verse we have concluded

that the manuscript evidence compels us to doubt it. We add here that the probabilities are more in favor of the verse than they are against it. Such scribal boldness is possible, but it has very rarely been demonstrated; and Luke's patterns of thought are a valid piece of evidence.

Chapter Seventeen

INTRODUCTION TO JOHN

The Importance of John's Gospel

If Jesus Christ were known to us only through the Gospel of John without the additional insights of the Synoptic Gospels, how would we think of him? There would be no Nativity stories; and while we have seen that these accounts raise historical questions, at the same time they help to put Jesus in the world of historical experience. There would be no Sermon on the Mount. There would be fewer miracles; and, as we hope to set forth in this commentary, the miracles reported would have a different significance. There would be no parables; in particular, we would not know such classic parables as the Good Samaritan and the Prodigal Son. We would not know the Twelve, and we would know nothing of the slowness of understanding which the Synoptic Gospels in varying degrees affirm of them. We would not know Matthew the publican nor Zacchaeus the publican; and we would not know that Jesus was called a friend of tax-collectors and sinners. It is probably no exaggeration to say that Jesus, known only through the fourth Gospel, would appear to be a visitor from another world. Many Christians think of him as such a visitor anyway; and behind this thought is the belief, not formally expressed, that a visitor from another world has very little to tell us about this world. All this may suggest that the Gospel of John needs the Synoptic Gospels more than the Synoptic Gospels need John.

Christian devotion and Christian tradition have never found an irreconcilable opposition between the Jesus of the Synoptics and the Jesus of John. This was and is the response of faith; but it was also the response of an uncritical readiness to ignore the differences, a rather shallow and imperceptive reading, and a fear of what recognition of the differences might involve. In modern times the principles of history and of criticism do not permit students of the New Testament to ignore the differences nor to recoil from their implications. And it may as well be said at once that historical and critical study of the Gospels has given no one a reason to abandon his Christian faith. The questions which the fourth Gospel raise are primarily historical and critical questions; they are not really theological questions in the sense that the theology of the Synoptic Gospels and the theology of John are mutually exclusive.

The historical problem is centered on the sources of the Synoptic and the Johannine presentations of Jesus. The traditional thesis affirmed that both presentations came from eyewitnesses. Modern criticism has dulled this edge of the problem by attributing neither the Synoptics nor John directly to eyewitnesses. One can hardly escape the impression that if the Synoptics are "historical," John is less historical; and this impression is sustained by modern critics, whatever be their disagreement of the definition of the term "historical."

In the traditional thesis the fourth Gospel was attributed to John, the son of Zebedee, the brother of James, a Galilean fisherman. This tradition first appears in the writings of Irenaeus in the late second century, but Irenaeus attributes it to men of the early second century. The same tradition placed the composition of the Gospel in Ephesus in Asia Minor; another tradition which located the writing at Antioch in Syria was never widely accepted. The differences between John and the Synoptics were explained by the statement that the Gospel was written in John's old age, near the end of the first century; and the location of the writing in Ephesus permitted interpreters, ancient and modern, to see in the Gospel certain effects of John's residence in Asia Minor, effects which could be identified as Hellenistic patterns of thought not to be expected in the writings of a Galilean fisherman.

This identification is not found in the Gospel itself. Much has been made of the point that John, who mentions the names of eight of the Twelve more frequently than any other Gospel, does not mention James and John, the sons of Zebedee. But neither does he mention the names of Matthew and James "the Less." "The Beloved Disciple" (19:26; 20:2; 21:7, 20) is identified in 21:24 as the witness and the author of "these things." It is assumed that this means John; it is not certain that this is the meaning intended, nor that the editor was correct if this were the meaning he intended.

We should mention briefly some reason why the statement of Irenaeus does not carry conviction. One reason is that he attributes to Polycarp a personal knowledge of John the Apostle which Polycarp does not claim in his own writings. Another reason is his failure to distinguish clearly between John the Apostle and "John the Elder," mentioned by some other early writers. The evidence does not compel one to identify the apostle and the elder in order to distinguish them; the evidence simply does not allow a solution to the problem.

John and the Qumran Writings

A third reason is derived from the documents of Qumran. Comparison has shown that the Gospel of John has more affinities with the Qumran material than any other New Testament book. It is extremely difficult to suppose that these affinities all arise from the memory of an extremely old man forty to sixty years after his experience of the Qumran material. For the Qumran community was abandoned in 68 A.D., the year the manuscripts were concealed in the places in which they have been found since 1947. If we are dealing with John the Apostle, or indeed with any one of the Twelve, the personal contact of the author with the Qumran material would, it seems, have to be pushed back another thirty to forty years. This consideration should be taken together with the recognized fact that John knows the geography of Palestine better than the other evangelists, and that he is well acquainted with Palestinian Judaism, which historians are sure came to an end in the Roman war of 66-70 A.D. These considerations do not carry conviction; but they raise serious doubts both about the late date of the fourth Gospel and about its authorship in Asia Minor. It is just these two points on which the statement of Irenaeus depends. That the Gospel should have been written in Palestine does not argue against the authorship of John, but it does argue against the authorship of John as Irenaeus affirmed it. One recent writer, R. M. Grant, has put the writing of the fourth Gospel about the year 70, which would make it earlier than Matthew and Luke.

The Qumran affinities have led recent scholars to examine once again the alleged and long accepted Hellenistic themes and patterns of the fourth Gospel. As a result of the examination scholars are much slower to find that John derives very much from Hellenistic sources or that his Gospel is directed to Hellenistic Christians. His indebtedness to the Old Testament and the certain types of Jewish thought is much better established than his indebtedness to Greek sources; but it must be said that the sources of John remain a problem. Readers of the preceding portions of this introduction will have noticed that sources are a problem for all the Gospels. The peculiar aspect of the problem of John's sources comes from the fact that the Synoptic tradition is not among the sources of John. This has usually been explained by assuming that John either did not know the Synoptic tradition or chose to ignore it. The hypothesis of the authorship of an aged member of the Twelve makes ignorance an unlikely assumption; and one is then forced to think of reasons why John ignored or rejected the Synoptic tradition.

As we have mentioned, interpretation has generally and for a long time proceeded on the principle that the Synoptic Gospels are "history", or are closer to history, or are intended to be history; that, on the contrary, John is not "history," or is not as close to history, or is not intended to be history, whatever may be the definition of the word "history" in the statement of this principle. More recent interpretation has found that there is theology and symbolism in the Synoptic Gospels as well as in John, and that to distinguish John from the Synoptics on the basis of "history" is misleading. All the Gospels are documents of faith, which they both presuppose and explain. All are intended to motivate the statement of faith that Jesus is Messiah and Lord, a statement which historical observation alone does not motivate. The Christ event is not a mere fact of history.

Similarly, interpretation has generally treated the faith of John as more "developed" than the faith of the Synoptic Gospels, whatever this may mean. "Developed" as compared to "undeveloped" faith could refer to a development which occurs in time, but this too can be misleading. At any given moment of the history of the church there is "more developed" and "less developed" faith in the church, the faith of the hierarchy or of the theologians as opposed to the faith of "the simple." Yet all are and think themselves members of the same church, sharing the same faith. If John is more "developed," this need not mean that he is later in time; and in fact it would be difficult to show that the faith of John is evolved from the faith of the Synoptic Gospels, or from the Christ event as presented in the Synoptic Gospels.

The Development of Christology

The modern interpreter of John must face the possibility that the proclamation of John is more "developed" than the proclamation of the Synoptic Gospels, but that it is also "primitive" in the sense that it is early. This does not imply that the interpretation of John is based upon "the very words" of Jesus, nor upon the superficial observation of the events of the life of Jesus. It is a theme common to all four Gospels that faith with understanding was not achieved by the disciples until after the resurrection of Jesus. The Gospel of John may indicate that it took less time to achieve a "developed" Christology than historians have generally assumed. It will be our purpose both in the subsequent portions of these introductions and in the brief commentary to point out the most important features of the development.

The fourth Gospel gives the impression of a unified structure much more than the Synoptic Gospels do. It is somewhat paradoxical that modern interpreters are much more inclined to find displacements in John. If it is true that the structure of John is more rigorous, then it should be easier to recognize displacements; in most of the Synoptic Gospels there is little apparent reason why a passage should be in one context rather than another, and both Matthew and Luke on occasion alter the order of Mark. The major displacements suggested by scholars will be noticed in the proper places. In general the theory of displacement is based on the hypothesis that pages of the manuscript were arranged in the wrong order; that is, the displacements are not thought to be the deliberate work of scribes and editors. No suggested rearrangement imposes itself, and printed Bibles follow the order of the manuscripts. In quite recent years some manuscripts of John from the second century have been published; these manuscripts have the arrangement of the manuscript tradition, and any displacements must be placed extremely early. The fourth Gospel also presents a number of celebrated critical text problems, which will be mentioned in the proper places.

The Different Christs?

The study of the Gospel of John makes it necessary to

raise the question of different "Christs," and some readers
may find this disturbing; did not Paul mention "one Lord"
(Ephesians 4:5) among the symbols of Christian unity? If
the question is pursued, it leads into the celebrated antithesis between the Jesus of history and the Christ of faith;
and to many this phrase suggests an antithesis between
the real Jesus and the unreal Christ. Yet there is an un-
deniable difference between the Jesus of John and the
Jesus of the Synoptic Gospels; and we should explain that
this is not surprising, but inevitable.

Any person who ever existed is a historical reality in
the sense that he is the object of experience. But there is
hardly anyone whose personality is so simple that he is
known exhaustively by any one. Almost any man among
our contemporaries has several circles in which he lives:
his home and family, his business and his business associates, and probably a circle of close friends who are
neither family nor business associates. The same person
can manifest himself quite differently in these three circles;
and in fact most men prefer to keep the circles distinct.
He is the same person at all times, but the resources of the
human person are so rich that he may appear a complete
stranger in one role to a person who knows him only in
another.

This variety is compounded if a man becomes a public
figure, and especially if he becomes a historic figure. In
that case he becomes a person of some importance to
many who do not know him personally. An impression of
his person grows and is diffused which is based less on
personal acquaintance than on memories passed through
many minds and affected by the thought not of what he
was but of what, in his established historical role, he ought
to have been. Thus the historic person easily becomes
many persons; and historians may search for "the historical Abraham Lincoln" with problems similar to the problems of those who search for the historical Jesus. For it is
always true that the person who achieves historical im-

portance is a complex person whose total reality was probably never experienced by any one.

There was only one historical Jesus. If there were only one representation of the historical Jesus, we would know it was false; for the historical Jesus revealed to us in the Gospels is not a simple person. One may assert that the disciples knew him well after two or three years of close association; but we have had to point out that Mark emphasizes their recalling that they never understood him. This memory was too much for Matthew and Luke, but there can be no doubt that Mark's view of the disciples is primitive and accurate. It comes through even in Matthew and Luke; what is obvious in all three Synoptic Gospels is that none of their sources ever experienced anything like the Jesus of John.

Is the Jesus of John then unreal? Only if faith demands unreality for its object. The disciples did not experience the glorified Jesus; but they believed that he was glorified, that he was enthroned as Messiah and Lord. John really, and very probably beyond his intentions, presents the glorified Jesus. It is a presentation not unrelated to the "realized eschatology" mentioned in the introduction. Was the historical Jesus unimportant to John? Possibly he was, although it is difficult to find the words to say this properly, and we are not sure how well John knew the other Gospels. But these Gospels assure us that he presents a Jesus in whom the church believed, but whom the disciples had never experienced.

In the history of the church there have been many Christs; and we may again illustrate from Christian art. Artists have commonly preferred to represent the glorified Christ even in Gospel scenes; he is given a halo, for instance, and not infrequently the entire Trinity and angels are represented as visibly manifested. Many crucifixion scenes portray Jesus crucified with the serene dignity of a bishop celebrating pontifical solemn Mass. Obviously this is the Christ of faith and not the historical Jesus. The royal

Christ and the militant Christ of so many images are not only not the historical Jesus, they are not even the Christ of faith; often they are false Christs. When Christians represent him whom they call the Prince of Peace marching at the head of their armies, they proclaim a false Christ. When an artist attempts the crude realism of Goya or El Greco, he becomes offensive to the devout, even though such realism is far closer to the historical Jesus than the triumphalism of the Renaissance and the baroque Christs.

John falls into none of these faults. He presents the real Jesus transfigured, but not perverted into a symbol of conquest and rule. The Jesus of John proclaims the commandment of love as the one commandment, and leaves the washing of the feet as the last memory before the passion. In such features as these the Jesus of John is still too real for many Christians.

The Structure of John

The sublimity of the Gospel of John is a commonplace among interpreters which is readily accepted by readers. The Gospel seems to move on a heavenly plane, or rather to describe the encounter of the heavenly being with the earthly reality. The reader does not know that the sublimity which he accepts as a trait of the Gospel is achieved with the smallest vocabulary of all the books of the New Testament. Sublimity is achieved by the use of a few key words which evoke the mysterious. These key words are essential to the structure of Johannine theology; they come in opposites: life-death, light-darkness, truth-lie. Glory is a key word with no opposite. Knowledge is opposed not to ignorance but to unbelief. It has often been suggested that these opposites reflect some kind of dualism of early Gnosticism. By dualism is meant a system which reduces reality back to two original principles, one good and one evil. Gnostic dualism is defined by its belief that man is saved from death, darkness and sin by revealed knowledge. The Qumran material shows closer affinity with the Johannine opposites than any known Gnostic documents do; and in addition the Gnostic documents are later than John. The mythological image of a conflict between good and evil is not rigorous dualism, and such a conflict appears in John as it does not in the Synoptic Gospels. If John was not influenced by the Qumran material —an assertion which should not easily be made—he does reflect the same world of thought.

That world of thought can be recognized as ancient Near Eastern, which includes the biblical world. Life-death and light-darkness appear in the creation account of Genesis 1; the creator divides light and darkness and brings forth land and sea from chaos. The creation account of Genesis in turn echoes older creation myths of Mesopotamia. The Gnostic myths also came from the ancient Near East. Only in John does Jesus appear as the light and the life of the world; and as such he is a cosmic figure not known to the Synoptic Gospels.

When the "developed" Christology of John is mentioned, what is meant is John's clear belief that Jesus is the pre-existent Son of God who becomes incarnate. It is an exercise in futility to seek even an obscure expression of this belief in the Synoptic Gospels. Yet Paul, who is earlier than the Synoptic Gospels, likewise knows Jesus as the pre-existent Son. For this reason the word "developed" should not be taken as synonymous with "later." It is the absence of the developed Christology in the Synoptic Gospels which causes the problem rather than its presence in John. But in fact, modern theologians have no right to demand that a first century writer exhibit the most fully developed theology of his time. Modern writers do not always exhibit the most fully developed theology of their time, and reasons are not far to seek.

It must be admitted that the humanity of Jesus appears less clearly in John than it appears in the Synoptic Gospels. In early portions of these introductions we have noticed a gradual transfiguration of Jesus from Mark through Matthew to Luke. In John the process reaches its fullness; but, as we have observed, the process is also seen in its term in Paul. In one classic and difficult passage Paul appears to say that he is not interested in the humanity of Jesus (II Corinthians 5:16). This is probably not what he meant, but what he did mean is not clear. The emerging church in its documents does show a gradual diminution of interest in the "historical Jesus," to use a modern term; but it should not be thought that this attitude did not appear until the end of the first century. The purpose of John is stated (20: 31) in these terms: ". . . that you may know that Jesus is the Messiah, the Son of God, and that through faith you may possess life in his name." The title "Son of God" is known to the Synoptics, but they give no indication that they understood the title in the Johannine sense.

The structure of the fourth Gospel suggests an artificial arrangement. We have seen that the Synoptic Gospels are compilations of originally detached sayings and incidents. John arranges his material into a series of miracles and discourses. As we shall see, the discourses take up themes which the miracles symbolize. But the discourses are not pure discourse; they include debates with adversaries and questions asked by disciples. Both the form and the contents of the discourses are foreign to anything in the Synoptics; and no modern commentator would deny that the author of the fourth Gospel attributes his own patterns of thought and speech to Jesus. While we can rarely be certain that we have "the very words" of Jesus, the Synoptic sayings are thought to reflect the speech of Jesus with less transformation than the discourses of John do.

The miracles in John are usually called "signs." The meaning of this word in this usage has been extensively discussed. Certainly the word suggests evidence; and what we call the apologetic value of miracles is clearer in John than it is in the Synoptic Gospels. This means the value of miracles are demonstrative evidence that Jesus is what he claims to be. This value does not proceed by logic; the

Jews are quoted in the Synoptic Gospels as saying that Jesus worked miracles by the power of Beelzebul. The idea of evidence, however, is far from exhausting the meaning of "sign." The miracles show both that Jesus is Messiah and Son and the meaning of messiahship and sonship. In the Johannine presentation the signs are of such clarity that they leave no room for invincible ignorance. Those to whom the Messiah Son has revealed himself are inexcusable if they refuse to believe.

Realized Eschatology

The Synoptic Gospels have three forms of the eschatological discourse, which they locate in the last week of the life of Jesus. The Gospel of John has nothing of the sort; and the absence of this type of eschatology led a modern scholar, C. H. Dodd, to coin the term "realized eschatology" for John's brand of eschatology. The meaning of "realized" can be seen in such sayings as "He who hears my word and believes . . . has eternal life" (5:24) and "He who does not believe is already judged" (3:18). Such sayings suggest that the advent of Jesus is the finally decisive world event for mankind as a whole and for individual men. The sayings do not exclude "apocalyptic" eschatology such as the end-event described in the Synoptic Gospels, but such an end-event could be only the revelation of a decision already made. Whether it leaves room or not, John does not mention such an apocalyptic event. "Realized" eschatology creates a problem similar to the problem of the early Parousia, and it is met in much the same way; the first Christians do not seem to have envisaged the lapse of time and the course of history which lay before the church. Their awareness of time, like their awareness of space, was limited by the world of contemporary observation. Within this limitation realized eschatology, more clearly than any other New Testament eschatology, lays the decision of life or judgment on the individual person.

The reader of the Gospel may wonder whether this em-

phasis on the individual decision may not have its counterpart in a comparatively dim awareness of the church and
of the social character of salvation. The word *ekklesia* does
not appear in John, as it does not appear in Mark and Luke.
In addition, the believing group of John is singularly un-
structured, even compared to the believing group of the
Synoptic Gospels. The New Testament does not suggest
uniformity of structure in the apostolic church. Yet in
certain subtle ways the church is more present in John
than it is in the Synoptic Gospels. John has a number of
allusions to worship and the sacraments which are much
more explicit than any allusions in the Synoptic Gospels.
The sacraments which appear are baptism, the sacrament
of initiation, and the Eucharist, the sacrament of Christian
unity. These allusions will be seen in the course of the
commentary. The reign of God appears only in 3:3-5 in a
conversation about baptism.

John's Vision of the Church

Another subtle aspect of the church of John is seen in
the Johannine moral teaching. The Synoptic Gospels contain a large number of sayings of Jesus which are concerned with moral teaching and moral problems. Matthew's
Sermon on the Mount has collected many of these in one
discourse. Such moral discussions have their counterpart
in the rabbinical discussions reported in the Talmud, and
no one has ever doubted that such sayings and discussions
are true to life. As John has no parables, so he also has no
moral sayings. He more clearly and frequently than any
other New Testament writer reduces the morality taught
by Jesus to the single commandment of the love of neighbor. No doubt this single commandment needed, and needs,
particular explanations of particular problems, such as we
find in the other Gospels; John simply does not attend to
them. The centrality of the one great commandment is not
peculiar to John; we have seen its statements in the other

Gospels, and Paul said that he who loves his neighbor fulfills the whole law (Romans 13:8). The Johannine emphasis seems to make structures and teaching unnecessary, almost as if the writer were evoking Jeremiah 31:34: "There will be no further need for neighbor to teach neighbor." John sees the church simply as a worshipping community of love. This vision of the church was not reached in the apostolic church nor has it been reached since. It is unfortunate that so many members of the church have regarded the vision as foolishly impractical and therefore not an objective for which the members of the church ought to work.

Unlike the Synoptic Gospels, John usually calls the adversaries of Jesus "the Jews" rather than scribes, Pharisees, and priests. In recent times this has often been adduced as an example of anti-Semitism, and it has been suggested that new translations should substitute some other word. What the word might be is not clear; and paraphrasing will not obscure the fact that "Christians" (messianists) seceded from Judaism or were expelled from Judaism because Jews as a body did not believe that Jesus was Messiah. This is the fundamental difference of belief between Jews and Christians, the difference which makes other differences seem trivial. Nor can the fact be hidden that this difference of belief has often elicited conduct which had no foundation in the beliefs of Judaism or of Christianity. Recognizing that this has happened may help to assure us that it will not happen again. Other New Testament books reflect some of the bitterness of these early quarrels. That John does not make the distinctions which the other three evangelists make is something of a puzzle. Perhaps we cannot solve it, but in handling the puzzle it might be wise as well as fair to remember that the author of this work was himself a Jew, and that one of his sayings of Jesus is "salvation is from the Jews" (4:22). If anti-Semitism had never had any more support than it can get from the New Testament, and from John in particular, this aberration would have a much briefer history than it has had. It has been a disease of the western world; and its cure can be effected only by Christians and Jews together, not by Christians alone.

Gnosticism

A slightly fuller examination of the Gnosticism mentioned in the introduction is in order. Under this name are grouped several of the earliest heresies, most of which are not well-known. They are dualistic, as we have stated. Generally the evil principle of the universe is identified with matter, and the good principle with spirit. Thus the creation of the world is not the work of God but of the devil, and the fall of man does not consist in sin but in acquiring a body. The redemption of man consists in his dematerialization and his return to the state of pure spirit. In such a scheme redemption through Christ is difficult to explain; but obviously there is no room for an incarnation. Therefore Christ is the redeemer by bringing man knowledge, the knowledge which enables man to escape his body and to return to the state of pure spirituality. Most of the preserved Gnostic myths of redemption are highly elaborate and usually grotesque. The knowledge which the savior brings is occult and destined for only a few elect.

Some consequences of this scheme are obvious. It makes the supreme virtue consist in the avoidance of bodily activities and bodily pleasure. Some Gnostic sects renounced marriage as sinful. Christianity is turned into an extremely snobbish sect by Gnosticism. The gospel is not to be proclaimed to all men, but only to the few who are capable of understanding. The Jesus of the Gospels becomes unreal. Salvation is achieved not by love but by knowledge reserved to the privileged which culminates in pseudo-mysticism. The Christian is not obliged to do anything but merely to be passive; he has no obligation to others, for he could contribute only to their bodily welfare.

Little explanation is necessary to show that some traces

of Gnosticism have survived in the church from the earliest
centuries. Some exaggerated forms of Christian asceticism
have dealt with the body and its functions as if they were
sinful by definition. Certainly the search for pleasure can
and often does go beyond all reasonable bounds, but the
New Testament nowhere suggests that the refusal of all
pleasure is a work of love. Jesus seems to imply that life
apportions enough pain to test the love of every one. He
did indeed make fun of the rich fool, but he did not himself live like Lazarus. The cult of pain for its own sake
makes as little Christian sense as the cult of pleasure for
its own sake. The acceptance of pain can be much easier
to bear than the responsibilities of love.

Salvation through knowledge revealed to a few elect
has its echo in salvation through doctrine. Again, the New
Testament indicates that man is saved through the experience of love and not through the experience of learning,
and that an error of judgment is far more tolerable than a
refusal to love. The church has committed many sins in the
name of the sound doctrine which it felt obliged to preserve. It has been far more intolerant of doctrinal error
than it has been of failure to love. In this respect the church
has sometimes shown itself more Gnostic than Christian.
It has other duties to the neighbor than to provide him with
occult knowledge.

That the church has often exhibited a sectarian character
needs no demonstration. Where Jesus said, "Come to me,
all who labor and are burdened," his church has seemed
to say, "Crawl to me, all you who labor and are burdened,
and I will lay it to you." It has drawn firm lines of division
between the elect and the damned, and insisted that the
lines be maintained. In this generation we seem to be
seeing the end of the sectarian church. It is a hopeful development, and possibly it may compel the end of other
Gnostic relics.

Gnostics used knowledge in the Greek sense, the sense
in which we use the word. John used the word in the He-

brew sense, for which there is no exact English equivalent. It is clumsy to say that Hebrew knowledge was dynamic and experiential, but all these words seem necessary. The meaning of knowledge is perhaps nowhere better illustrated than in the idiom that a man "knows" his wife. It is also seen in the phrase that God "knows" some one in the sense that he has chosen that one and cares for him. Had this background of knowledge been recognized, Gnosticism would probably have made much less progress. In John knowledge is a vital union of possession which, when it is referred to man and God, is founded on faith and grows by love. It has none of the defects inherent in the Gnostic system of knowledge, which are still dimly perceived in the Gnostic traits of the contemporary church.

Chapter Eighteen

THE GOSPEL OF
JOHN, CHAPTERS 1–5

The Word of God

The difference between John's Gospel and the Synoptics is at once apparent in the *prologue (1:1-18)*. Instead of a reference to the nativity John affirms that Jesus is the pre-existent Son of God. The relation of sonship is expressed by the title "Word," used only here and in I John 1:1. The title alludes to the Old Testament "word of God," which has several aspects. As the creative word (frequent and especially in Genesis 1) it is the expression of power which brings all things into being; the pre-existent Son is identified with this word. It is also the revelatory word which brings light into darkness and life to the perishing. The Servant of the Lord is a "light of the nations" (Isaiah 42:6). Man lives not by bread but by God's utterance (Deuteronomy 8:3). This divine word is now revealed as a person who has "pitched his tent" (v.14) among men; the word probably alludes to the "tent" of the Levitical traditions in which Yahweh dwelt in the midst of Israel. The "darkness" suggests not only the cosmic darkness into which the creative light burst at the word of God, but the darkness of unbelief into which the word entered. This new word, or rather the original word now revealed with all clarity, is the word of grace and truth; the old word, obscurely spoken, was the word of the Law, not the word of grace and truth.

The *witness of John (1:19-34)* is given with much greater clarity than in the Synoptic Gospels. The disciples of the

Baptist endured as a distinct group well into the second half of the first century, and all the Gospels make it clear that John was the precursor of the Messiah, not the Messiah. In this passage the Baptist denies any messianic qualities at all, even the role of Elijah or of the pre-messianic prophet, both of whom were expected in Judaism to announce the Messiah. The question of why John baptizes has a background which modern learning has not yet discovered. In John's gospel the vision of the baptism is a revelation to John the Baptist. The title "Lamb of God" is also obscure; it may identify Jesus as the Passover lamb of the new exodus, but the language may also allude to Isaiah 53:4-7.

The call of the first disciples (1:35-51) cannot be combined with the Synoptic accounts of the call, all of which are located at the Sea of Galilee. Here Andrew calls Peter; the new name of Peter is placed here. The Synoptic tradition was uncertain about the conferring of the name— except Matthew 16:18, the only source which gives an explanation of the name. The unnamed disciple in this passage has often been identified with John the son of Zebedee. Philip and Nathanael are identified only by John; Nathanael is usually identified with the otherwise unknown Bartholomew of the Synoptic lists. The remark of Nathanael suggests that Nazareth had a bad reputation, but this suggestion is unsupported elsewhere. Nazareth is not mentioned in the Old Testament or in Jewish literature.

The miracle of Cana (2:1-12) is explicitly said to be the first of the "signs" worked by Jesus. No parallel to this miracle is found in the Synoptic Gospels; and the symbolism of the incident sets the tone for the Johannine treatment of miracles. The extremely large amount of water for ritual purification suggests the entire Jewish system of Law and cult. When Jesus orders the jars filled, however, the water acquires a different purpose; it has become the water of baptism, the Christian rite of initiation. But the water becomes the object of supreme wonder; the wine into

which it is turned suggests the wine of the Eucharist. Thus
the wedding feast becomes, with the insight of faith, the
revelation of the Messiah who saves through baptism and
the Eucharist, the cultic participations in his own life. The
wedding feast is an anticipation of the messianic banquet,
a theme known both in the Old Testament and in the
Qumran literature, and applied by early Christians to the
Eucharistic supper.

The mother of Jesus is mentioned here (2:1, 3-5, 12) and
in 19:25; in neither passage is her name given. The dialogue between Jesus and his mother is difficult. The address "woman" is not discourteous, but extremely formal
for a son speaking to his mother. The words used by Jesus
have parallels elsewhere, and they always signify dissociation or refusal. The "hour" in John is the time of the manifestation of Jesus, and can refer either to his crucifixion
or to his glorification.

The cleansing of the temple (2:13-25) is found in all four
Gospels, but John places it at the beginning of the ministry
of Jesus. Only John associates the incident with the saying
about the destruction of the temple, known to Mark and
Matthew.

The conversation of Jesus with Nicodemus (3:1-21) is
one-sided; Nicodemus has an opening sentence and two
bewildered questions which do not advance the discourse.
The topic of the discourse is baptism, a rebirth to a new
life which is an absolute necessity for entry into the kingdom. This is a birth of the spirit and the saying echoes the
appearance of the spirit at the baptism of Jesus. The discourse of vv.11-21 does not continue the topic of baptism;
it affirms the coming of the pre-existent Son as the bringer
of life. The play on the word "lift up" (v.13), alluding both
to crucifixion and glorification, is used later in the Gospel;
John means to merge the two events as the other Gospels
do not. "Realized eschatology" appears in the passage; the
decision of belief or unbelief itself accomplishes life or
judgment.

The witness of John (3:22-36) is the final statement of the Baptist that he must disappear with the coming of the one he announces. The continuation of the discourse in 3:31-36 can hardly be attributed to the Baptist, and many think it is displaced. It affirms again the pre-existent Son, with particular reference to his exclusive knowledge of the Father, whom he has seen and heard. In virtue of his knowledge as Son he has a total and exclusive commission to communicate eternal life.

Jesus Preaches to the Samaritans

The preaching of Jesus to the Samaritans (4:1-42) is peculiar to John; the Synoptics know of no ministry to the Samaritans. That Jesus should open the conversation with a Samaritan woman was surprising both because he was a rabbi and because she was a Samaritan. The situation at Jacob's well (a famous landmark which still furnishes water) permits a discussion on the theme of water (once more; see chapters 2-3). There is a play on the words "living water," which normally meant fresh and running water; Jesus turns it to mean the water of eternal life (see Isaiah 55:1; 58:11), an allusion to the regenerative waters of baptism. The woman, embarrassed by Jesus' knowledge of her personal life, turns the conversation to cult, meaning sacrifice; both Jews and Samaritans agreed on one place for sacrifice, but disputed its location. The answer of Jesus implicitly abolishes sacrificial worship and replaces it with worship "in spirit and truth"; the phrase is obscure, but it clearly signifies that this worship can be offered anywhere. The Christian reader would recognize the allusion to the Christian cult. The simple affirmation of messiahship has no parallel in its clarity elsewhere in the Gospels. The return of the disciples elicits a saying about the harvest which must refer to the apostolic church rather than to the situation of Jesus and the disciples at the moment. The Synoptic Gospels must be right in knowing of no mission of Jesus to the Samaritans. They are symbols of the pagans,

rejected and condemned by the Jews, who show a faith in
the Messiah of the Jews that is denied by his own people.
When the disciples proclaim the good news and are believed, they reap the harvest which Jesus has sown; for the
Son is the revealer.

The cure of the official's son (4:43-54) has certain affinities with the cure of the centurion's slave in the Synoptic
Gospels; but the Gentile identity of the official is not
affirmed. The point of the faith which accepts the mere
word of Jesus is found in John's version as well.

Work on the Sabbath

The cure of the sick man (5:1-47) occurs at a place in
Jerusalem with a name that is confused in the MSS.;
Bethzatha seems to be the best reading, but Bethesda as a
name of hospitals is established in English usage. The remains of a porticoed building which suits this description
have been discovered in Jerusalem. The angel who moved
the water is not found in the most important MSS. (5:3b-4).
It is not the cure but the removal of his pallet by the cured
man which institutes a dispute about Sabbath observance,
a common theme in the Synoptics. The response of the
sick man implies that one who can cure permanent disability can also dispense from the Sabbath observance. The
long discourse (19-47) is not concerned with Sabbath
observance, but with the meaning of the catchword
"work," derived from the prohibition of work on the
Sabbath. According to Genesis 2:2-3 God himself rested on
the Sabbath after creation. This was interpreted by the
rabbis as a permanent rest, a world Sabbath. Jesus affirms
another point of view; God's work in saving and judging
is never ended. The Father has commended this work to
the pre-existent Son. Jesus claims no power to work independent of the power which the Father has given him;
but Jesus' power is as full as the power of the Father himself. The exercise of this power is stated again in terms of

realized eschatology. Yet the work of the Son is more apparent in the resurrection than it is in the judgment. He calls men to rise to a life which they already have; if they do not have life, their judgment is already accomplished. This theme will reappear more explicitly in the account of the resurrection of Lazarus.

The relation of Father and Son as set forth in this passage is the foundation of later developments in Trinitarian and Christological belief and theology; it is not identical with these later developments. Much of the discourse seems to be a refutation of the charge that Jesus claimed to be equal with God (v.18). This is met by affirming that the Son can do nothing independently of the Father. Later theology found it necessary to refine this statement by a distinction between person and nature which John did not know.

The discourse goes on to appeal to the witness of John. As in the Synoptic Gospels, it is plain that the Jewish authorities were unable to reject John. In addition to the witness of John, Jesus appeals to the witness of his own works, the works which the Father has given him (v.36). The witness of the Father himself can only be the witness of the Scriptures with which the discourse concludes. The messianism of the Old Testament is mentioned frequently in the New Testament; but we know little of the primitive Christological exegesis of the apostolic church. It would be difficult to identify the text of the Pentateuch which John has in mind when he says that Moses wrote of the Messiah.

Developed Christology

We have used the phrase "developed Christology," and certainly one is entitled to ask what this means. The reader has probably been long accustomed to think of the faith of the church as one set of simple truths handed down from the apostles; and we certainly risk confusing him when we say it is something else. But we cannot speak of the Christology of John without pointing out that we have in John a way of speaking of the relations of God to God, whom he called his Father, which is different from the speech of the Synoptic Gospels. We must add that it took the church hundreds of years to arrive at a way of speaking of these relations which are not heretical, and that her speech has never been entirely safe from ambiguity.

The New Testament writers could not have said that Jesus Christ is God; God meant the Father. They could and did say that Jesus is God's son. This phrase admits much closer definition; fatherhood and sonship in a context of theological discourse must signify a different reality from the reality signified by these words when they are used of human beings. What more can be said of the reality signified, at least to make clear the difference between divine sonship and human sonship? The earliest great heresy assumed that God could be a father only by creation, and that his son is therefore a creature. The church rejected this statement of Arius, but it did not find another statement with which it could live comfortably for over a hundred years.

Pastors and theologians know that the majority of Catholics either are not interested in such questions or they have gross misunderstandings which are impossible to remove entirely. Hence we should not really be surprised that the language of the Synoptic Gospels about this problem is so casual. The authors of Matthew, Mark and Luke were, it seems, no more capable of asking questions about divine fatherhood and sonship than their readers were. It is altogether impossible to deduce the Nicene Creed, and still less the dogmatic statements of the Council of Chalcedon from the Synoptic Gospels. Did their authors not know or care that Jesus Christ is God from God, Light from Light, true God from true God, begotten not made, consubstantial with the Father? The word "consubstantial" had not even been invented yet; far from defining it, the evangelists could not even have spelled it. No, they did not know and they did not care.

John introduces a new element of interest and of concern. He has an awareness of the problems implicit in the designation "God's son" which we do not find in the Synoptic Gospels. Certainly he intended to remove any suggestion of carnal generation; and we must remember that in the religious world both of the ancient Near East and of Hellenism the ideas of divine fatherhood and sonship were commonplace in mythology. One scholar entitled his collection of Canaanite myths "The Loves and Wars of Baal and Anath;" and the amours of Zeus and Apollo have been immortalized both in poetry and in art. For a Jew the use of such language was impossible.

We point out in the commentary that John goes back to the Old Testament for a word to describe the relations of father and son which does not imply carnal generation. Jesus is called the Word of God; and it is evidence of the aptness of this designation that it has become common, although it occurs in only two New Testament passages, in the Gospel of John and in the First Epistle of John. In the Old Testament the spoken word, even the word of men, is conceived as having an enduring reality of its own. It is a thing laden with power and with revelation, each measured by the power and the knowledge of the speaker. It is an extension of the personality of the speaker. The word of God is obviously laden with a greater quantity of power and of revelation than the word of man. It endures forever; it has the eternity of the speaker. It cannot be frustrated, for it has his power. The fullness of the word of God is revealed as a person who dwells among man and is a man among men.

Certainly, as we have noticed several times, something of the experience of the historical Jesus is lost when this emphasis is placed on his sonship and his identity as God's final word. For the insight into the historical Jesus we depend on the Synoptic Gospels, especially on Mark. But with the four Gospels the Christian faith assumes the form which it retained. The Christian faith can say nothing about Jesus unless it affirms his relations both with the

Father and with other men. It has been difficult, and at
times one element has been emphasized at the expense of
the other. It remains a mystery on which the last word has
not been uttered.

Chapter Nineteen

THE GOSPEL OF JOHN, CHAPTERS 6–11

The Loaves and the Fishes

The multiplication of the loaves and the fishes (6:1-15) is the only miracle which is surely common to all four Gospels. John adds such details as the words of Philip and Andrew; and he alone mentions the psychological effect upon the crowd. This detail is in fact discordant with the Synoptic account that Jesus dismissed the crowd; John needs the presence of the crowd for the discourse which is occasioned by the miracle. All four Gospels have echoes of liturgical formulae in the narrative; John's is the giving of thanks and the distribution by Jesus himself. *The walking on the sea (6:16-21)* is found in Matthew and Mark.

The discourse on the bread of life (6:22-71) is located in the synagogue at Capernaum, but the location comes almost as an afterthought (v.59). The first words of Jesus take the offensive; the interest of the crowd is actually selfish and materialistic. The only work which God imposes upon them is faith. The request for a sign seems singularly out of place in this narrative context; such inconsistency is of course possible, but we are reminded that the discourses of John are artificially constructed. Jews did indeed regard Moses as the great wonderworker; Jesus, compared with Moses, had given ordinary bread and not the unfailing manna from heaven. Jesus responds that God, who gave the bread of life to their fathers, also gives them the bread of life. Jesus himself is this bread; life is communicated by faith in him. To the objection that Jesus,

191

whose family is known, cannot be the bread that comes down from heaven, Jesus responds somewhat indirectly that no one can believe this unless the Father draws him to believe. The meaning of "life" is reaffirmed; this bread from heaven does not merely sustain human life through its normal course, which is all that the manna did; but it is the bread which defeats death.

Only with v.51 does it become clear that the bread of life is the flesh of Jesus; and the eating and drinking is meant literally, not merely as a metaphor of faith. Some think that John has joined two discourses, but the development in the revelation of bread of life is consistent. Not only faith but the Eucharist is necessary to defeat death. The affirmation is not qualified and many refuse to believe any longer. The last line includes the words of Jesus as sources of spirit and life. The faith of the disciples expressed by Peter corresponds to the confession of Peter in Mark and Matthew.

The discourses of the feast of Tabernacles (7:1-52) are broken up by interlocutions, but maintain a loose unity of themes as well as a unity of time and place. The kinsmen of Jesus appear here in a character similar to their character in Mark 3:21; here they manifest not simple unbelief, but unbelief in the true character of Jesus. Jesus dissociates himself from their plan for display and appears late at the festival with no fanfare. The first saying of Jesus again takes the offensive; he affirms his mission from the Father and charges the Jews with lawlessness because of their desire to kill him—the first time John has introduced this theme. The saying presupposes only the cure of chapter 5; yet 7:31 implies a number of "signs." Jesus not only reaffirms his mission from the Father but his return to the Father in the future. This prediction was simply misunderstood.

The final saying of Jesus once again introduces the theme of living water, alluding to the water of baptism. The quotation in 7:38 exists nowhere in the Old Testament. The final discussion of the chief priests and Pharisees is actually a summary of their erudite unbelief; and John makes the point that in addition to the leaders, others were profoundly impressed.

The adulterous woman (7:53-8:11) is simply not found in any early MS. and was unknown to the Greek Fathers. The theme of forgiveness of the sinner contrasted with Pharisaic harshness is common in the Synoptic Gospels; but with the MS. evidence, the passage cannot be the work of the author of the fourth Gospel.

A series of debates with the Pharisees follows. The saying about the light (8:12-20) echoes the prologue of the Gospel. It leads to another dispute about the credentials of Jesus. Once more he appeals to the Father, this time by a rather subtle use of the Mosaic law requiring the testimony of two witnesses. The Jews do not know the Father and therefore his testimony will never reach them. The severity of this denial that the Jews do not know the true God mounts in the course of the disputes contained in this chapter. The warning against unbelief (8:21-30) again affirms the pre-existent Son and his mission from the Father. By a word play on "lift up," meaning both crucifixion and exaltation, Jesus makes his death and resurrection the ultimate "sign."

The dispute about Abraham (8:31-59) is more or less unified by the catchword Abraham. The antithesis of freedom and slavery reminds one of the epistle to the Galatians: but whereas Paul wrote of slavery to the Law, John wrote of slavery to sin. The boast of descent from Abraham is rejected, as it is rejected in Matthew 3:7-10 and Luke 3:7-9; Romans 4; Galatians 3:6-29. The Jewish claim to perpetual freedom is difficult to explain. Jesus denies that they are children of Abraham or of God; they are children of the devil, the liar and the murderer. This must surely be the climactic invective of all the Gospels. Jesus asserts his own innocence and the vindication which the Father will give him. This leads to a clear assertion of

preexistence, and his life is threatened for the first time.
The preexistent Messiah actually does appear in rabbinical literature; and it was also rabbinical belief that the
patriarchs and Moses saw the Messiah in a vision.

Blindness and Unbelief

The cure of the man born blind (9:1-41), peculiar to John,
is the second sign performed by Jesus in Jerusalem. The
question of the disciples presupposes the ancient wisdom
doctrine, set forth by Job's friends, that illness and mis-
fortune are punishments; the absurdity of a punishment
for personal sin inflicted at birth passes unnoticed; but
the idea of collective guilt is entertained. The answer of
Jesus merely touches on another explanation of suffering—
that it is a means by which God reveals himself. Saliva
is used in the cures of Mark 7:33; 8:23. The inquisition
which follows is a dramatic dialogue in which the growing
faith of the man marches parallel with the growing unbelief of the Jews. Faith and unbelief each grow with
successive steps by the consideration of the same evidence.
In the concluding sayings it becomes clear that there is a
self-willed blindness which cannot be cured except by the
confession that one is blind. Congenital blindness is assumed to be the most difficult form of the affliction to
cure, but it is not. The blindness which refuses to see God
at work is worse, and it strikes only those who wish to be
struck. Expulsion from the synagogue for belief in Jesus
Messiah is a practice introduced by John into the life of
Jesus from the experience of the primitive church in the
latter years of the first century. "Son of Man," less frequent
in John than in the Synoptic Gospels, is a messianic title.

The discourse on the good shepherd (10:1-21) is not actually a parable, although it is often called one; the parables of the Synoptic Gospels are stories. The Greek word
which is translated as "parable" in 10:6 is not the Greek
word used to designate the parables of the Synoptic Gospels. "Shepherd" is an ancient royal title, not only in the

Old Testament but also in earlier Near Eastern civiliza-
tions. As Jesus uses the figure it does not suggest royalty
but rather the shepherd of Psalm 23, who is Yahweh. The
features of the shepherd are mutual recognition—which
can be verified in modern times wherever sheep are herded
—and dedication even to the risk of life. This is more
surprising; but the dangers of the shepherd's life are mentioned by Jacob (Genesis 31:38-40) and David (I Samuel
17:34-37). The reference to a single flock is indeed applicable to church unity, the application usually made in
modern times; but the original saying means the Gentiles,
as the sheep, are not yet gathered into the one flock. By
rather loose association the reference to the danger of
death leads to a clear affirmation that Jesus met death by
his own decision; the decision which no man has about
himself was within the power of the pre-existent Son. The
response of the Jews, as in chapter 8, was divided between
favorable and hostile.

Feast of Dedication

The discourse of the Feast of the Dedication (10:22-42)
begins with a demand for a clear affirmation of Messiahship. Such an affirmation is reported only in the conversation with the Samaritan woman; with the Jews Jesus
presents his credentials ("signs") and affirms not Messiahship but commission from the Father. The statement of
unity with the Father, which here brings the threat of
stoning, has already been made in language no less clear
(5:19-23; 8:58); in the latter passage stoning was threatened. A claim to be the Messiah was not a claim to be God.
Jesus evades the charge of blasphemy by a rabbinical
argument; even in the Scriptures the noun "god" is used
of human beings. The exegesis of Psalm 82:6 is not in
question here; no Jew could believe that the line was
addressed to any but human beings. Jesus then reaffirms
that he has an intimacy with the Father shared by no human being; and the final statement of 10:38 appears almost

as an acceptable revision of the more daring statement of
10:29. The withdrawal from Judea is not called a withdrawal from immediate danger until 11:8.

The resurrection of Lazarus (11:1-44) is not found in the
Synoptics; neither is Lazarus, although Luke mentions
Martha and Mary. The absence of the episode in the Synoptics is most easily and frequently explained by the
symbolic character of the miracle in John. Of all the
resurrection stories this is the only one in which a man is
raised from the tomb; the story thus anticipates the resurrection of Jesus himself. Lazarus is buried in the same type
of tomb and he is "of four days" (11:39); the number
corresponds to the reckoning of three days and three nights
for the sojourn of Jesus in the tomb (Matthew 12:40; Mark
8:31; 9:31; 10:34). Jesus, usually serene in John, shows
profound human emotion at the grave, enough to elicit
remark. The resurrection and the life saying returns to the
theme of Jesus as life; (see the prologue and chapter 6). It
also expresses realized eschatology. Death and burial for
one who believes have a meaning different from the meaning of normal experience. The believer who dies actually
lives in the eternal life which he has received through
faith. The Lord of life has only to address him and he rises
with the life which is in him.

The plot to kill Jesus (11:45-54) is attributed to the chief
priests and the Pharisees. The saying of Caiaphas is "pro-
phetic" in the sense that it is ambiguous, saying more than
the speaker intends. This "fuller sense" is attributed to
divine inspiration.

Signs vs. Miracles

John, more frequently than the other Gospels, calls the
miracles of Jesus "signs"; and he exhibits a somewhat different attitude towards the miracles. The word "sign" in
the Old Testament often indicates some evidence that God
is at work. It need not be a miracle in the modern sense of

the word, but it means an event enough out of the usual
to draw attention to itself. It can resolve a doubt; the request of the Jews for a sign (Mark 8:11) is made in the
same sense in which Isaiah offered Ahaz a sign (Isaiah
7:11). The slightly different attitude of John is seen in his
generally favorable use of the word; in Mark 8:11 (and its
parallels) Jesus treats the request for a sign as evidence of
obstinate unbelief and refuses it.

Thus it would seem that John's idea of sign is not far
from the modern theological idea of the demonstrative
value of miracles, an idea which has become archaic.
While the miracles of the Synoptic Gospels are less obviously "significant," they do nevertheless reveal a reality.
The miracles of the Synoptics reveal Jesus as savior (and
here we recall that the Greek word translated "save"
means "heal"). By miracles Jesus gives food to the hungry,
drink to the thirsty, health to the ill, movement to the
crippled, life to the dead. He does "wonders" of which
John says that the beliver will do greater wonders (14:12).
It is short-sighted to think of the Synoptic miracles as being simply feats and not to see the revelation of the will
to do good to men in need. These deeds are revelations of
the power and will of God to save. The deeds are continued
in the church; the church cannot imitate the feats, but it
can be the instrument of the saving power and will of God.
Active love is the working power in the church which
signifies the presence and work of God.

These considerations may help to show that John's understanding of "sign," or rather of what is signified, is not
the same as the other Gospels. The number of wonders is
small—six; in some instances, not clearly all, they seem to
be selected because the element of wonder is heightened.
Thus the blind man is blind from birth, the paralytic has
been crippled for thirty-eight years, and Lazarus is not only
dead but buried and decaying. This does not obscure the
power to save, but one gets the impression that attention
is drawn to the power more than to the saving.

Another feature, more difficult and too large for proper treatment here, is that only two of John's miracles have parallels in the Synoptic Gospels. Older explanations that the Synoptics did not know of these or had reasons for not mentioning them are simple evasions. The Synoptic authors did not know of these miracles, and modern scholars are compelled to ask if they did not know of them because they did not happen, at least in the manner described. If John transfigured the words of Jesus, why should he not have transfigured his deeds also? John was not concerned with the probative value of historical fact; this is not what "sign" means. He was concerned with the sign as a symbolic revelation of the reality of Jesus, and it never occurred to him to attribute to Jesus a power which Jesus did not have.

It is possible, perhaps not without a bit of contriving, to relate John's signs to some of John's major themes. In these signs affirmations are made about Jesus which have no parallel in the Gospels or in the Epistles. Jesus is called the way; this is signified in his restoration of the power to walk (chapter 5). He is called the light; this is signified by his gift of sight to the men who never had it (chapter 9). He is called the life; he gives the means of sustaining life (food, chapter 6; drink, chapter 2), strength at failing life (chapter 4), life after death (chapter 11). That we have four signs in one category and one in each of the others may support the view that this interpretation is contrived; but the suggestion does illustrate the incontrovertible principle that John's signs are revelations of the Johannine Christ. To some degree, even though the miracles of John remain saving acts, they are "spiritualized," whatever this cumbersome word may mean. The healing of the paralytic suggests the crippling of sin. The loaves and fishes lead the believer to seek the Eucharistic food and drink of eternal life. The man born blind sees, but the spiritual blindness of the Pharisees is incurable. The "real" resurrection of Lazarus is his resurrection to eternal life. This "meaning"

of the signs does not depend on the brute historical factu-
ality of the report; and one can understand how John
transfigured the events of the early gospel traditions. He
moves in his own area of discourse, where his readers have
not always followed him.

Chapter Twenty

THE GOSPEL OF
JOHN, CHAPTERS 11–16

The Last Passover

The conspiracy against Jesus (11:55-57) is described in an atmosphere of rising tension and popular interest in Jesus. *The anointing at Bethany (12:1-11)* is found in Mark and Matthew; Luke includes the anointing but in a different time and place (7:36-50). Traditional interpretation has somewhat unfairly identified Mary of Bethany as the repentant prostitute of Magdala. The critic of the action is identified in John as Judas Iscariot, the first ecclesiastical treasurer. The saying of Jesus is perhaps the closest parallel between John and Mark-Matthew. John and Luke have the anointing of the feet, a rather unrealistic occurrence; the anointing of the head for banquets and festive occasions (see Matthew 6:17) described by Mark and Matthew was normal.

The description of Jesus' entry into Jerusalem (12:12-19) is again close to the Synoptic version; the lowly messianic king of Zechariah 9:9 is a denial in action of secular messianism. Only John mentions the palms which have given the name to Palm Sunday; and it is puzzling because the palm does not grow in Jerusalem. John maintains and emphasizes the theme of popular admiration; here, as frequently, John distinguishes between the Pharisees (or the priests) and the general Jewish population.

The prediction of the death of Jesus (12:20-36) is given in response to the Greeks, who are mentioned and then forgotten. "Greeks" must mean Gentiles who had accepted

Judaism. Death and glorification again are not clearly distinguished; the word play on "lifted up" is used once more (32; see 3:14; 8:28). The saying about the grain of wheat has no real parallel, but 12:25 is close to the Synoptics (See JB margin). The saying in 12:27-28 corresponds to the Gethsemane episode of the Synoptics; but hardly any interior struggle is suggested. The heavenly voice is parallel to the voice at the baptism; John evidently means to distinguish between those who can discern the voice of God and those who hear only a clap of thunder. The concluding saying on light echoes the prologue and chapters 8-9; it is intended to represent the final public appeal of Jesus. *The concluding saying (37-50)* is a summary. The unbelief of the Jews is described in the quotation from Isaiah 6:9-10, used also in the Synoptics; and popular belief in Jesus is again affirmed. The sayings of Jesus (12:43-50) are almost entirely repeated from earlier discourses; the themes are light, judgment and the commission of Jesus from the Father.

John's account of the Last Supper (13-17) is much longer than the Synoptics, by the addition of several discourses, but it lacks the institution of the Eucharist. It is clearly the day before the Passover, but in the Synoptics it is the Passover supper; there is no satisfactory explanation for this discrepancy. *The washing of the feet (13:1-20)* is another employment of the symbolism of water, but not of baptismal water. The washing of the feet signifies the fellowship of humble service within the community. The act and its explanation are parallel to Luke 22:24-30 (see parallels in Mark 10:42-44 and Matthew 20:25-27). The veiled allusion to domestic quarrels becomes clearer in the following section. *The foretelling of the betrayal of Judas (13:21-30)* contains an explicit (if cryptic) identification of the traitor know only to "the beloved disciple." Such an identification is unknown in the Synoptic Gospels, although they have the phrase "dipping the hand in the dish" in another meaning. Nor do the Synoptics have the

departure of Judas at this point. John, who has no Gethsemane scene, had to give Judas time to accomplish his
betrayal; but John does know the garden (18:1) although
he does not use the name Gethsemane. *The saying about
glorification (13:31-32)* treats the glorification as already
begun, since the treason of Judas initiates the passion. *The
new commandment of love (13:33-35)* is a theme which is
repeated in this series of discourses. Love within the community is not in opposition to the love of one's enemies
(Matthew 5:43-48) nor is it a lower ideal; it looks to the
establishment of the community of love which embraces
all of mankind who desire to enter it. *The prediction of
Peter's denial (13:36-39)* is parallel to the Synoptic account.

The first part of the farewell discourses can be called
the discourse on the Father (14:1-31). The Father is not
really a unifying theme but rather the topic to which the
discourse returns. In 14:31 an invitation to depart is issued
which is not fulfilled until 18:1; many critics think the
original discourse, limited to chapter 14, has been expanded. In the first place the return of the pre-existent
Son to the Father is affirmed. This is a motive for peaceful
confidence. The saying about many rooms is obscure, but
it seems to say that there is no reason to fret about place
and position; they will follow him. Thomas' question
shows befuddlement, and it elicits the statement that Jesus
is the one way to the Father (whom to know is to live;
see 17:3). This leads to the question of Philip, and in turn
to a new affirmation of the intimate relation of the Father
and the Son, here described in the word "indwelling,"
which has since become a technical term in theology. And
since Jesus does his works by virtue of the indwelling, the
faith which unites the believer to Jesus produces in the
believer the power of wonderful works.

The commandment of love is restated in isolation, and
the spirit is promised as "advocate"; so very probably the
word *parakletos* should be translated, although "consoler"
has also been suggested. The return which Jesus promises

is not clearly the Parousia of the Synoptic Gospels, but rather the resurrection. It is the commandment of love, which creates the indwelling of Father, Son and believers. This theme is restated after the question of Judas. The Advocate now appears as a teacher and indeed after the manner of a rabbinical teacher; the words of Jesus are the sacred text which the Advocate will interpret. A celebrated problem in Christology is found in 14:28; and it is perhaps best to say of this verse that there is much about the relation of Father and Son which we do not know. The "prince of this world" is Satan, who took possession of Judas Iscariot in 13:27, the incarnation of the "world" as the power of sin opposed to the Father and to Jesus. He has no real power; but death, freely accepted by Jesus, is a part of the reign of sin and death.

The Commandment of Love

The discourse on the vine (15:1-17) echoes Israel, the vine of Yahweh (Hosea 10:1; Isaiah 5:1; Jeremiah 2:21). The figure of the vine is often compared to the Pauline image of the body. The emphasis of the figure falls upon the dependence of the disciples upon Jesus, a dependence which demands the indwelling. The discourse then turns to the commandment of love. The fulfillment of this commandment secures the indwelling. The friendship assured by the revelation of the plan of the Father is implicitly contrasted with the Jewish assurance based on the knowledge of the Law.

The discourse on the world (15:18-16:4) employs the term "world" in a sense peculiar to John in the New Testament; from the Johannine writings the word has passed into Christian, particularly Catholic usage in much the same sense. The world is not nature but the world of men; this does not mean mankind in general—not, for instance, the mankind which is ripe for the harvest (4:35). It is not even mankind as sinful, fallen and unregenerate. It is men who refuse to believe even after they have heard

—one could say before they have heard—because they already have a total and irrevocable commitment to the world. They are men hostile to God and to Christ; the hostility may be latent, but when God reveals himself through Christ the hostility becomes active. The Advocate now appears as a witness; he bears witness through the witness of the disciples. The idea is similar to the idea of Matthew 10:20; Luke 11:11-12. The references to persecution reflect the experience of the early church. The reference to those who kill the disciples in the service of God seems to allude to Jewish persecution rather than Roman persecution. In fact Christians themselves have fulfilled this saying as often as it has been fulfilled upon them. When the church becomes a community of hate rather than a community of love, it becomes "the world" in the Johannine sense.

Coming of the Advocate

The discourse on the Advocate (16:4-15) establishes a connection between the return of the Son to the Father and the coming of the Advocate which is obscure; much Trinitarian speculation has proceeded rather inconclusively from this statement. The Advocate now appears in the activity his title indicates; he proves the world wrong under three categories. The three points, traditionally translated as "sin, righteousness and judgment" are well rendered in the Jerusalem Bible, but the interpretation is still somewhat obscure. That the prince of the world is "already condemned" does not readily appear as evidence for the Advocate's argument; the "world" had not collapsed at the glorification of Jesus, and one wonders what manifest judgment John had in mind. The Advocate again appears as a teacher and interpreter, and it is stated still more emphatically that Jesus alone is the revealer of the Father. The Spirit is meaningless unless the Word has been spoken first. It has long been taught in theology that the personal reality of the Spirit is more clearly announced in these discourses of John than in any other passage of the New Testament. This may be conceded, but "personal reality" did not mean to John what it means to more recent theologians.

The discourse on the return of Jesus (16:16-33) again refers to the resurrection rather than to the Parousia; in John resurrection means glorification. The analogy of the pangs of birth is conventional; yet there are allusions in Jewish literature to cosmic disasters which were expected to precede the apparition of the Messiah, called "the birth-pangs of the Messiah." The theme of petition in the name of Jesus, briefly mentioned earlier in the discourses, is now amplified; it is related to the theme of power—the disciples will have power to do works as great as the works of Jesus. Finally, the disciples are promised clarity both of revelation and of understanding; they have come to believe in the pre-existent Son who now returns to the Father. The disciples rejoice somewhat prematurely in their knowledge, and they are warned that within a few hours they will abandon Jesus. All the Gospels place this prediction in the pathetic context of full professions of undying fidelity. The final verse is a statement of complete victory already accomplished; this is a "realized eschatology."

If chapters 15-16 are compared with chapter 14, a degree of repetitiousness appears which is surprising even in John (who is often repetitious). The hypothesis that the last discourse is actually two or three variants of the same discourse cannot be demonstrated, but it has to be mentioned. The composition of these discourses is different from the composition of the other discourses of John. The hypothesis of variants may not explain the composition, but it is an attempt to solve a problem which is there.

The Last Discourse

The center of interest in this portion of the fourth Gospel is the "last discourse" of Jesus (14-16). We have mentioned

very briefly some of the literary problems of the compilation of this discourse; but neither the allotted space nor
the conclusions of scholars permit us to advance beyond
uncertainity in these problems. It does, however, seem
worthwhile to draw attention to some of the striking differences between this discourse and the teaching of Jesus
in the Synoptic Gospels. We have observed that much of
the Synoptic teaching is moral; the only moral teaching in
this discourse, as indeed throughout the fourth Gospel, is
the commandment of love. In the Synoptic Gospels Jesus
uses parables and concrete examples; in this discourse we
move above the level of the concrete. And we have the
outline of the Johannine church, to which I wish to draw
particular attention.

The church, as far as John develops the idea, can be
summed up in the word "indwelling," which we have
mentioned in the commentary. This word has antecedents
in the Old Testament and in Judaism. Yahweh dwelt among
his people in the ark and in the temple. Ezekiel (11:22-23)
pictures the symbolic end of this dwelling; when Yahweh
leaves, the city falls to its enemies and is destroyed. John
does not clearly locate the indwelling in the group; in fact
14:23 is more easily understood of the individual than of
the group as a whole. In general John is more conscious
of the relation of the individual believer to the Father and
the Son than other New Testament writers are. But this
does not alter the suggestion—one can hardly call it a
picture—of the community consisting of Father and Son
and believers who "dwell" in each other. "Indwelling"
rather than "dwelling together" seems to be not an inexact
use of language but an attempt to express a reality for
which the language has not been invented.

Such a community is as loosely structured as one can
imagine while still calling it a community; and one will
find no more structure elsewhere in the Johannine writings.
The parable of the vine really says no more about structure; basically it is another statement of indwelling. John

speaks of the life of the church rather than of its structure. In this discourse one feels that his point of view is better described as mystical than theological; not many New Testament writers exhibit a mystical outlook. The mystical outlook does not exclude structure; if the traditional date of John is correct, the writer lived at a time when the church had acquired a much more complex structure than we can find in the New Testament. The structure flows from the life, not the life from the structure. With this tribute having been paid the church's structure, one must confess the impression that John cared nothing about the structure.

Into this indwelling a third element is promised, the Spirit. This discourse has always been the main source of Trinitarian theology, Trinitarian meaning that theology which establishes the Third Person; there has never been any difficulty about the Father and the Son. But the spirit of Yahweh in the Old Testament is clearly impersonal, and quite often the spirit in the Gospels and the Epistles is mentioned in Old Testament language. Luke, Paul and John are the New Testament writers in whom the Spirit becomes prominent. John shares Luke's understanding that the Spirit is given only after the glorification of Jesus. Paul who thinks of the church as the body of the Risen Christ, also thinks of the Spirit as inspiring the church; and the Pauline view rather than the Johannine view appears in most Catholic theology and liturgy. Since there is no clear relation between Paul-Luke vs. John, we can conclude that there were at least two streams of theology of the Spirit in the primitive church, and that they resembled each other substantially. Much of the resemblance, of course, comes from the common biblical source. Among the Old Testament forms of the spirit is included the charismatic impulse which moved men to speech or action beyond their known capacity and expectations. Clearly the Spirit in both John and Paul is charismatic. The Spirit is also charismatic in Matthew 10:19-20 and Luke 12:11-12; but one really cannot reach a personal being in such texts any more than one can in the Old Testament.

In John the Spirit is certainly a sequel of Jesus, to use a neutral word; Trinitarian theology abhors words like "dependent." The Spirit cannot come until Jesus has been glorified. As we point out in the commentary, Jesus is the teacher, the Spirit is his interpreter. Outside of this the Spirit does not have the charismatic qualities of the Spirit in Luke and Paul. Strangely it is Paul (Romans 5:5) who identifies the Spirit as the principle of love within the Christian; in John, the Gospel of love, the Spirit is rather a principle of understanding. Here, John must reflect the theme of Mark, which we have seen weakly echoed in Matthew and Luke, that the disciples really never understood Jesus before the charismatic enlightenment of the Spirit.

Chapter Twenty-one

THE GOSPEL OF
JOHN, CHAPTERS 17–21

Jesus Prays

The prayer of Jesus (17:1-26) has been called the priestly or the high-priest prayer since the sixteenth century, although it contains no reference to specifically sacerdotal functions. "The hour" which has come is, once again, the hour of passion and glorification. Eternal life is defined in realized eschatology as the knowledge of the Father and the Son; the unity of the two, affirmed in several contexts, here means that the Father can only be known in the revelation of the Son (14:9). The depth of faith and understanding which is attributed to the disciples is out of harmony not only with Mark and, to a lesser degree, with Matthew and Luke but even with other contexts in John—for example, the questions asked by the disciples in chapters 13-16; the artificial discourses of John often ignore the contexts in which they are set. That Jesus does not pray for the world is understood in the Johannine sense of "world"; since the world is by definition mankind opposed to God, Jesus can only pray that it will cease to be the world. It can then be included in the prayer for the disciples which follows.

The first petition in the prayer for the disciples is that they may remain outside the world, although "outside" does not expressly mean physical departure. They remain outside the world because the Father protects them from "the evil one." The translation "the evil one," who is "the prince of this world" (14:30), is preferable to the neuter "evil." The disciples are consecrated in the truth, which means to the truth. The truth is the word of Jesus which reveals the Father. The prayer for unity of the disciples presents the unity of the Father with the Son as a model for the disciples' unity with each other; and it also makes the unity of the disciples the condition for their complete unity with the Father and the Son. The bond of this unity is not merely a bond of common purpose or of close co-operation, but the bond of love. Thus the new commandment becomes equivalently the constitution of the church, the dwelling place of the Father and the Son with men.

John's narrative of the passion goes much its own way; but there are similarities with the Synoptic account, and John certainly relates the same event. *The arrest of Jesus (18:1-11)* is to be placed in Gethsemane, although John does not use the name. There is no mention of the agony (see 12:27); Jesus is superior to such human emotions as fear. Jesus is also superior to the arresting force, to which John has strangely (and doubtfully) added a detachment of Roman soldiers (the cohort, v. 3). It is scarcely relevant to discuss whether this included the entire complement of the cohort, normally 600 men. The mere affirmation of identity throws them flat on their backs, and leaves no doubt that Jesus is not overpowered. Only John identifies the defender of Jesus as Peter and gives the name of the servant as Malchus.

The account of *the hearing before Annas and Caiaphas (18:12-27)* is not the account of a judicial process. Unlike Luke, John makes room for not only one inquiry, but for two; but John has no legal process before the Jewish council either at night or on the following morning. Commentators remark that for John's theological purposes and considering the time he wrote, it was no longer of interest to know on what charges Jesus had been condemned; Jews refused to accept him as Messiah and Son of God, and it was for these claims that he died. If this be the theological significance of John's omission, the omission oversimplifies history. The triple denial of Peter is interspersed in the narrative; as in the Synoptics, the series of denials is initiated by the question of a servant girl.

The first hearing before Pilate (18:28-40) begins with another indication that John places the event on the eve of Passover; but some scholars question whether the laws of ritual cleanliness were as rigorous as 18:28 indicates. Again no charge is laid against Jesus; even when Pilate is described as asking a direct question about the charge, there is no direct answer. If it is agreed that for John's theological purposes the charge was not important, it is not without interest that the charge is nowhere in the Gospels quoted directly, and it is quite possible that when the Gospels were written the charge was no longer known. Questions are also asked about the right of Jewish authorities to execute capital sentences; the problem is still obscure. In none of the Gospels is there any doubt that sentence was passed and executed by Roman officers under Roman law.

The quality of the charge is implied by the dialogue of Jesus and Pilate concerning kingship; the dialogue implies a charge of rebellion against Rome. In all the Gospels, except for this passage, the claim of messianic kingship is so subdued as to be never clear. At the point of "glorification," in the double meaning which John gives the word, the claim can be made and defined. The Christian church was not going to deny Jesus the title of king, but the kingdom is the kingdom of "truth." This is represented as being clearly beyond the interest and comprehension of Pilate, and also as understood by him to be entirely non-political. A solid part of the evangelical tradition of the passion is that the Roman judge found no case against Jesus. The Barabbas incident is barely mentioned by John; possibly he, like modern commentators, found it difficult to explain.

Jesus is Tortured

The second hearing before Pilate (19:1-11) is separated

from the first by the scourging; in John, as in Matthew
(27:27-31), the scourging is not clearly motivated. Commentators have long interpreted it as an effort on Pilate's
part to save the life of Jesus by submitting him to a lesser
punishment; this is possible, but it must be judged imaginative. The display of Jesus as mock-king is a step in the
"glorification" which John describes; the unworldly king
is acclaimed without understanding, as Caiaphas without
understanding explained the death of Jesus (11:49-50).
Some scholars point out that the words of Pilate represent
the Aramaic, "Here is the Son of Man." The Jews' statement of the claim of Jesus leads to another dialogue, but
Jesus refuses to discuss the charge.

In regard to the political pressure applied to Pilate,
John's report of *the condemnation of Jesus (19:12-16)* is
clearer than the Synoptic version. The threat of a secret
denunciation to the emperor has great historical verisi-
militude; by means of such denunciations the Romans
maintained their imperial administration, and in fact Pilate
himself was removed from office a few years later through
such denunciations. Writing shortly after the fall of Jerusalem if not much later (in any hypothesis), John reports
the Jewish profession of allegiance to Caesar with supreme
irony. They reject their king who comes to save for a king
who destroys them.

The crucifixion (19:17-22) is reported with continued
emphasis on the theme of kingship. John makes the kingship of Jesus the official reason for his execution, even
though the Jews refuse his kingship. *The division of the
garments (19:23-24)* of the condemned was a normal per-
quisite of the executions. The seamless robe is very probably a midrash on the psalm quoted; and the robe may be a
symbol of the unity of the church, for which Jesus had
prayed. Only John mentions the presence of the mother of
Jesus (still unnamed) at the crucifixion. Symbolism may
indeed lurk in *the words of Jesus to his mother (19:25-27)*;
if it does, it is obscure. The position of the childless widow

was desperate, and perhaps no more than this fact is needed to explain the words. *The death of Jesus (19:28-37)* is related with a generous amount of midrashic interpretation, even (as in 19:28-29) of a psalm text which is not quoted. The last word of Jesus in John is a declaration of the completion of the work; the Son dies with a clear awareness of what he has accomplished. Hastening the death by the breaking of the legs is an attested practice; it was not done to Jesus, and this also becomes the occasion of the midrash. Most commentators see the sacramental symbolism of baptism and the Eucharist in 19:34; the author evidently regards the fact as important. In the account of *the burial (19:38-42)* John diverges from the Synoptics in placing the anointing of the body here; he thus removes the motivation for the visit of the women to the tomb, and reports the visit of only one woman.

In the account of *the empty tomb (20:1-10)* John has replaced the women with Mary Magdalen, but has added Peter and the beloved disciple as witnesses, somewhat parallel to Luke 24:12. *The apparition to Mary Magdalen (20:11-18)* is also roughly parallel to the apparition of the women in Matthew. *The apparition to the disciples (20: 19-29)* is suggested by Luke 24:36-43. Thus this chapter has an unusual number of similarities with the Synoptics. John, however, makes this apparition the occasion on which Jesus confers the Spirit, the Advocate of chapters 14-16, and the episode thus corresponds to Luke's Pentecost. The power of the disciples to forgive sins does not specify the penitential discipline, neither does it exclude it; the power is given in quite general terms, and may be thought to include the powers of preaching and healing as well as sacramental powers. The unbelief of Thomas becomes the occasion of the most explicit profession of Christological faith in all four Gospels. The narrative clearly signifies that this early Christian acclamation was pronounced with as much assurance by Christians as it was by one of the twelve.

The Conclusion of John

The conclusion (20:30-31) is meant to end the entire Gospel; it states the purpose of the book. What follows is the appendix (21:1-23), probably added by an editor. The story of the miraculous catch of fish (21:1-14) has obvious resemblances to Luke 5:4-10, but the sequel differs. Hence commentators have sought some symbolism in the number of fish; and the author must have been aware of the saying about "fishers of men," which he does not use. The editor in 21:14 intends to connect this episode with the preceding chapter. The genuine purpose of the appendix seems to be to affirm the primacy of Peter (21:15-19) among the disciples; it corresponds to Matthew 16:17-19 and Luke 22:31-32. The Johannine treatment of the theme (meaning by Johannine a school if not the same author) characteristically makes the primacy of Peter a primacy of love and not of faith, as it is implicitly stated both in Matthew and in Luke. The image of a shepherd applied to Peter recalls the good shepherd of 10:1-18. The second purpose of the appendix is to explain away a popular belief that the beloved disciple would not die before the end. This does not identify the beloved disciple as John, and tells us nothing about him except that this popular belief existed.

The second conclusion (21:24-25) affirms that the beloved disciple is the source (not necessarily the writer) of the Gospel; and leaves room for the other Gospels.

The World

In the latter chapters of the fourth Gospel there is frequent mention of one of the common Johannine themes, the world. The use of the term in something like the Johannine sense has long been common among Christians, who are warned against the world, assured that they are not of this world and should not be; and certain misunderstandings can arise. In the rest of the New Testament the world sometimes appears in a cosmological sense, meaning either the visible universe or the inhabited earth; neither of these uses is common in John. More frequently the world means the human race; and in this sense it is rarely theologically nuetral, for mankind is usually seen as fallen and alienated from God. The world has its own spirit, its own kingdom, its own rulers.

This theological meaning of world appears in John as a sharply polarized opposition between God and the world. Sinful mankind is seen as a kind of anti-God, an enduring reality which is neither saved nor capable of salvation. In that sense Jesus does not pray for the world (17:9). This enduring reality, however, does not fall irresistibly upon individual men; they are saved by departing from the world. Neither Jesus nor his disciples are of the world in this sense.

As in some other themes, the language of John does not escape ambiguity. The world is the object of the saving act of the Father; and the mission of the Son is a mission to the world, of which he is the light (1:9, 3:19, 8:12. 9:5, 12:46). Because God loves the world he gave his only Son that the world might be saved (3:16-17). The world is hostile to God, but God is not hostile to the world. In such phrases the world does not cease to be sinful mankind; it is exactly sinful mankind which stands in need of the love of God and of God's saving act. God loves his enemy, and by his love he makes the enmity one-sided.

The ambiguity is not purely in the mind of John, nor in his language; the ambiguity is basically in the world, which adopts an irrational posture before God. God, instead of meeting hostility with hostility, meets it with love, a love which allows the hostility to kill the only-begotten Son. Instead of victory God seeks reconciliation. But reconciliation means the end of the world in the Johannine sense. To return to a theme treated earlier, the world ends when the Father and the Son and the believer dwell in each other. In this way Jesus overcomes the world; it cannot turn him into itself.

The Roman historian Tacitus, writing in the second century, relates the burning of Rome in the reign of Nero and the charge of arson laid against the Christians by Nero, which Tacitus did not believe. But Tacitus was not sympathetic to Christians either, and he remarks that many found it easy to believe the charge because Christians were popularly accused of "hatred of the human race." This is an inaccurate paraphrase of John's use of the theme of the world. Not to yield to the world has often meant to be narrow and intolerant, or to preserve some merely external distinction from other people in manners and customs. When Jesus said that his kingdom is not of this world (18:36), it obviously meant that he made no claim to political rule in the world of mankind. That claim which Jesus explicitly renounced has not always been renounced by his followers. When Jesus said that he had overcome the world, he had exhibited no political or military power whatsoever; John is consistent with himself in this passage and in the dialogue of Jesus with Pilate. Jesus overcame the world by his death, a type of conquest which his followers have not always been quick to imitate.

Thus Christian unworldliness has often degenerated into mere hatred and vindictiveness. It has degenerated into a desire to rule, to impose one's will rather than to reconcile by love. It is not the fault of the fourth Gospel that this has been the Christian attitude. It is a paradox that the Gospel of love should become the occasion of the gospel of hatred; and it suggests that there is no language of faith which cannot be perverted to support unbelief. For failure to accept God's love of this world and the gift of his Son is unbelief; to come between any one and this love and this gift is a basic work of unbelief. It is a denial of the saving act of God to restrict it to the elect; and to deny God's love of the world is ultimately to deny the reality of God and of his Son. Tacitus was sharper than he knew when he said that some had observed "hatred of the human race" in Christians. It takes no sharp observer to detect that it is still there.